Soviet and East European Studies

FOREIGN TRADE CRITERIA IN SOCIALIST ECONOMIES

FOREIGN TRADE CRITERIA IN SOCIALIST ECONOMIES

BY

ANDREA BOLTHO

CAMBRIDGE

AT THE UNIVERSITY PRESS

1971

Published by the Syndics of the Cambridge University Press
Bentley House, 200 Euston Road, London N.W.1
American Branch: 32 East 57th Street, New York, N.Y.10022

© Cambridge University Press 1971

Library of Congress Catalogue Card Number: 78–121366

ISBN 0 521 07883 0

Printed in Great Britain
at the University Printing House, Cambridge
(Brooke Crutchley, University Printer)

To My Mother

1570986

CONTENTS

[vii]

PREFACE

The material published in the following pages stems basically from a thesis submitted to Oxford University and substantially finished by the end of 1965. Some hasty bringing up to date was attempted during the summer of 1969. Changes were, however, kept to a minimum. Not much happened between those two dates in most of the Eastern European countries that could have fundamentally altered the body of the work. And as for the August 1968 'events' in Czechoslovakia, it is still too soon to judge what their effects will be on the economic life of that country, and notably on the process of economic reforms that had been so vigorously launched before the Soviet invasion. The word 'socialist' in the title has been kept despite the author's growing misgivings about, and disenchantment with, the countries to which it is applied. The only justification for it being maintained is that the strict economic definition of socialism still applies to the centrally planned economies examined. But in its wider and fuller sense, socialism seems to be fading away in Eastern Europe. It can only be hoped, following Isaac Deutscher (*The Socialist Register*, 1968), that one of the by-products of the economic reforms that are being introduced will be that of shaking the authoritarian and conservative political structures in power.

My greatest debt for whatever may be of any value in this work goes to Michael Kaser, my thesis supervisor. My research would not have been possible had I not obtained a scholarship from Nuffield College, Oxford. I would like to thank the Warden and Fellows for the opportunity they gave me to spend two years in the College's interesting and rewarding atmosphere. I owe a good deal to the help and suggestions of Francis Seton and feel also indebted for discussions and encouragement to V. Joshi, R. Portes and A. Hone. But I bear all the responsibility for the, no doubt numerous, errors that may still exist. Finally, this work would probably never have seen the light had it not been for the admirable typing of Mrs Carol Till, and the patience of my wife.

Paris, September 1969   A. B.

INTRODUCTION

The accession to power of new political régimes in Russia in 1917 and in Eastern Europe after 1945 brought with it a radical change in the economic systems that had so far existed in those countries. Varying forms of a market economy at differing stages of development were replaced by a centrally planned economic mechanism which, within a relatively short time-span, nationalized most means of production, abolished the role of prices as indicators of relative scarcity and allocated to itself the power to decide on practically all macro-economic issues and on many micro-economic ones.

Planning of some kind or other had already existed in capitalist economies before the establishment of communist power in Eastern Europe, either in the form of a rigorous centralization of decisions in wartime (e.g. Imperial and Nazi Germany, or 1939–45 Britain), or in the form of more general directives given by governments in order to stimulate some strategic branches of the economy (e.g. Bismarck's Germany, Witte's Russia, post-1860 Italy and, to a lesser extent, France). But these forms of planning strictly limited any encroachment on the private ownership of the means of production. The abolition of the latter in the Eastern European countries and the substitution of a central planning board for the individual role of the entrepreneur marks the great difference between capitalist and 'socialist' forms of planning.

The definition of socialism is, of course, ambiguous. From Babeuf to Lenin (and now Mao Tse-tung), the term has come to mean different things to various people, and the vague Marxist definition: 'from everyone according to his means, to everyone according to his abilities'[1] (as opposed to the future communist state when needs and not abilities will be rewarded), can be hardly taken as a point of reference by which to judge contemporary societies. But putting aside the broader social and political issues as to what is a socialist society and restricting oneself to the necessary, though not necessarily sufficient, economic conditions which can be considered to be indispensable

---

[1] K. Marx, *Critique of the Gotha Programme*, London 1933, pp. 29–31.

for socialism to exist, it can be argued with Lange that the
'socialization' of production (as opposed to the socialization of
production and consumption) is a *sine qua non* of a socialist
economy.[1] More specifically this implies the public ownership
of the means of production together with freedom of choice for
individuals in both consumption and occupation.[2]

The economic systems adopted in the Eastern European
countries can be said to fit these very broad terms of reference.[3]
It is true that freedom of choice in consumption and occupation
has been limited for a certain time (and to a significant extent
in certain cases), but given the relatively underdeveloped state
of the countries in question at the time the communist governments came to power, the democratic ideals implied in the
Lange definition were hardly attainable. The socialization of
the means of production, and the determination by the state of
the share of national income allocated to investment, had far-
reaching consequences on the institutions, organization and
working of the economic systems of the Eastern European
countries. No attempt will be made in this book to look at the
theoretical and applied economic developments which have
followed the establishment of socialist economic planning.
Attention will be focused on one aspect only of the economic
systems in question, namely that of foreign trade and, more
specifically, on the planning methods devised in order to substitute for the individual import and export decisions of private
firms the centrally co-ordinated decisions on international
trade in the absence of a market mechanism.

The changes in planning methods which will be examined

---

[1] O. Lange and F. M. Taylor, 'On the Economic Theory of Socialism', in B. E.
Lippincott (ed.), *On the Economic Theory of Socialism*, University of Minnesota
1938, p. 73.

[2] Ibid. pp. 72–3.

[3] Eastern European countries are hereafter defined as the following European
countries with a centrally planned economy: the Soviet Union, Bulgaria,
Czechoslovakia, the DDR, Hungary, Poland, Rumania and Albania (though
the latter is hardly ever considered). Other countries with a similar system of
economic planning are not examined here, either because the establishment of a
socialist régime in such countries is too recent (Cuba), or because the stage of
development reached by them is, as yet, so low that their foreign trade problems
are very different from those of the Eastern European countries (China, North
Vietnam, North Korea) even when their links with them are quite close (Outer
Mongolia), or, as in the case of Yugoslavia, because their planning methods and
economic history have been, over the last twenty years, very different.

INTRODUCTION 3

took place at a time when the foreign trade structure of the Eastern European countries was also undergoing rapid change. At the outset, Russia and the other centrally planned economies were relatively well integrated in the world economy, given their lower stage of economic development. The beginning of the Five Year Plans period for the Soviet Union and of the 'Cold War' for the smaller Eastern European countries led to an increasing degree of autarky together with the diversion of a shrinking volume of trade from traditional partners to other communist countries, especially the Soviet Union, with which previous trade flows had often been very small. While the drive to autarky was subsequently abandoned, the diversion of trade has been by and large maintained. Together with this sudden change in direction came changes in the commodity structure of trade. Before 1917, or 1945 according to which country is considered, the Eastern European countries enjoyed almost constantly favourable trade balances, thanks mainly to large exports of agricultural products.[1] Since the beginning of centralized planning, data on balance of payments have not been available for any of the Eastern European countries, and any estimate of their present balance of trade situations is consequently difficult to make. Rough adjustments that could be applied to their trade figures would tend to give the impression of relatively balanced trade, but this stems inevitably from their commercial policy, very often based on bilateral, or even barter, agreements. It can be argued, however, that in a more 'real' (as opposed to a purely 'accounting') sense, the Eastern European countries are in fact in a position of trade deficit which would manifest itself very quickly if larger financing possibilities were available. Such an argument would also be in line with the opinion, often reiterated in Eastern Europe, that import needs are in fact much larger and are

[1] Thus Russia 'generally had a favourable balance of trade in the years immediately before World War I', F. D. Holzman, 'Foreign Trade', in A. Bergson and S. Kuznets (eds.), *Economic Trends in the Soviet Union*, Cambridge, Mass. 1963, p. 285; Czechoslovakia 'over most of the inter-war period...had a sizeable export surplus', A. Zauberman, *Industrial progress in Poland, Czechoslovakia and East Germany—1937–1962*, London 1964, p. 271; in Poland 'over the last fifteen pre-war years surpluses of exports over imports were twice as large as deficits', ibid. p. 274; the same holds true for Hungary, Bulgaria and Rumania: J. Marczewski, *Planification et croissance économique des démocraties populaires*, Paris 1956, Vol. I, pp. 57–9.

suppressed only because of the limited availability of exports. As for the structure of exports, though agricultural commodities, and primary products more generally, are still very important, manufactures are rapidly increasing their share in the total, at least in the less-developed countries of the group.

Had the structure and direction of the Eastern European countries' foreign trade remained fairly similar to that existing before the introduction of a socialist economy, the adoption of centralized planning might not have created too many insoluble problems in the field of foreign economic relations. But in fact the upheaval of domestic institutions and of the domestic economy were accompanied by very large changes in the function, direction, weight and structure of foreign trade, so that entirely new theories and ideas had to be formulated to face the new problems. The present paper attempts to look at some of the ideas and theories which economists, in both East and West, have put forward to solve the foreign trade problems in the specific conditions of the centrally planned economies.

Two theoretical propositions existed when centralized planning started in Eastern Europe. One was an ideologically motivated adoption of Marxist economic principles embodied in the Labour Theory of Value (Chapter 1). An attempt to introduce this concept was in fact made and the results of this are still visible in the Eastern European countries, but the application of labour values to the field of international trade was never pursued, not even in trade between the socialist countries themselves. The second was the welfare economics solution suggested by Lange and Lerner (Chapter 2) which, theoretically, would have combined all the advantages of a market economy with those of planning. The political and economic conditions of the time were such, however, that the Lange–Lerner model could never have served as a basis for the economic decisions of Eastern European planners, either in the domestic or in the foreign trade field. It is only recently that ideas are evolving towards the sort of mixture of centralization and decentralization which was envisaged by Lange and Lerner in the late 1930s.

The lack of any applicable theory of international trade in a socialist economy was not felt too severely, as long as the

Soviet Union was the only centrally planned economy. Soviet planners groped for some *ad hoc* methods which, given their new foreign trade institutions (Chapter 3), would allow them to obtain the few indispensable foreign commodities they needed for their development plans (Chapter 4), and during the thirties and forties Soviet economic thinking was almost entirely devoted to internal growth problems. The wholesale application of Soviet planning methods to the other Eastern European countries had much more serious consequences for the foreign trade and economic development of those countries. By the middle of the 1950s the tensions created by an enforced state of near-autarky in economies formerly highly dependent on foreign trade reached a breaking point. Since that time the *ad hoc* foreign trade planning techniques of Soviet Russia have been replaced by new criteria, basically linked to comparative advantage principles (Chapter 5). The progressive development and refinement of such criteria, in a world in which relative prices have little bearing on many economic choices, have gradually led to the adoption of mathematical techniques and notably linear programming models which, thanks to shadow pricing, can displace the imperfect planning tools used in piecemeal analysis (Chapter 6). The next stage would logically be that of finding similar global criteria for application on the wider plane of the Council of Mutual Economic Assistance (CMEA).

In the meantime, the role of foreign trade in a socialist economy has changed quite radically. From an auxiliary to a domestic-led growth process it has become an inherent part of present growth efforts (Chapter 7), and the renewed importance it has acquired is bound to reinforce the links between the economies of East and West and of the less-developed countries. The Eastern European countries together accounted for perhaps one-third of world industrial output in 1968 but for only some 10 per cent of world trade.[1] As a United Nations document stated, 'this fact [i.e., relatively high share in world industrial production, relatively low share in world trade], combined with the plans of these countries for a continuing process of rapid economic expansion indicates the possibility of a much higher volume of trade with the rest of the world than exists

[1] United Nations, *Monthly Bulletin of Statistics*, June 1969.

at the present time'.[1] Even if, as will be argued in the Conclusion, the process of integration in Eastern Europe is carried further and intra-CMEA trade continues to represent, in the foreseeable future, a high and possibly increasing share of the trade of the centrally planned economies, this does not rule out the possibility of a much larger volume of trade with both industrialized and less-developed countries. The present economic reforms, with their double aim of increasing efficiency and therefore encouraging exports, and raising the share of national income going to consumption, thereby providing a further need for imports, would seem to point in this direction.

[1] United Nations, *Towards a New Trade Policy for Development* (Report by the Secretary-General of the United Nations Conference on Trade and Development), New York 1964, p. 90.

1

THE MARXIST APPROACH TO THE FOREIGN TRADE PROBLEM

Both for internal and international purposes, the necessity of some kind of value calculation for a socialist economy has been affirmed and reaffirmed by opponents and defenders of socialism alike. Engels, for instance, wrote: 'even then [i.e. under socialism] it will still be necessary for society to know how much labour each article of consumption requires for its production. It will have to arrange its plan of production in accordance with its means of production, which include in particular its labour power'.[1] And in the 1930s much of the controversy on a socialist economy was centred on the problem of value and was eventually settled by affirming the necessity of some such category in a collective economy.[2]

Granted, therefore, that for rational economic calculation it is necessary to use some value (or price) system which reflects the relative worth of commodities to the economy, the question which a socialist country had to answer was whether this worth was to be estimated in keeping with Marx's analysis, according to which goods, by the fact of having been produced by human labour, have some kind of intrinsic value linked to this labour, or whether, following the later developments of economic theory, it could be determined by the interaction of demand and supply forces (irrespective of whether these were to be allowed to work themselves out in actual markets or would just be simulated during the elaboration of a national plan). In the first case, the labour theory of value, as developed by Marx, has to be at the basis of the calculations and, in theory at least, the prices of commodities will reflect their labour values. In the second case, prices can be left free to be determined either by spontaneous market forces, or by the interaction of the market

---

[1] F. Engels, *Anti-Dühring*, 2nd edition, Moscow 1959, pp. 426–7.
[2] F. A. von Hayek (ed.), *Collectivist Economic Planning*, London 1938; Lange and Taylor, 'Economic Theory of Socialism'.

and planners' decisions or, finally, by total centralization. Once prices have been determined in one of these two ways, the flows of international trade (planned or spontaneous) will adjust themselves to the international price structures so determined. The first alternative will be examined in this chapter. Variations of the second case will be looked at in subsequent ones.

The labour theory of value

For Marx, then, commodities, abstracting from their 'use-value', 'have only one common property left, that of being products of labour',[1] which is, therefore, their only measure of value. This theory is defined in greater detail as follows: 'We see then that that which determines the magnitude of the value of any article is the amount of labour socially necessary, or the labour-time socially necessary for its production',[2] where the labour-time socially necessary is defined as 'that required to produce an article under the normal conditions of production, and with the average degree of skill and intensity prevalent at the time',[3] and labour itself is reduced to 'homogeneous human labour, expenditure of one uniform labour power'.[4] Given, therefore, that the value of a commodity at any given time and place is the amount of living and embodied labour necessary for its production, Marx argued that prices would in the long run conform to these values, even if in the short run fluctuations of demand and supply might cause some temporary deviations from them. In Volume I of *Capital*, the analysis is developed 'as though the law of value were directly controlling for the prices of all commodities'.[5] In Volume III, to take into account the varying 'organic compositions of capital' (the ratio of constant capital to the sum of constant and variable capital: $c/c+v$), assumed to differ in more advanced stages of capitalism between firms and sectors, Marx brings in the concept of 'price of production',[6] but the gist of the analysis is not really altered, even though Marx himself committed some errors when examining the relations between value and the newly introduced price

[1] K. Marx, *Capital*, Moscow 1961, Vol. I, p. 38.
[2] Ibid. p. 39.   [3] Ibid.
[4] Ibid.
[5] P. M. Sweezy, *The Theory of Capitalist Development*, London 1946, p. 109.
[6] Marx, *Capital*, Vol. III, p. 156.

of production. There is no need to go into the literature on these errors, the so-called 'transformation problem', but solutions to it 'have shown that a system of price calculation can be derived from a system of value calculation'.[1] The main defects of the labour theory of value do not stem from some apparent contradictions between Volumes I and III of *Capital*. Nor can it be argued that Marx ignored utility or demand and supply forces in his analysis of value. As for utility, he states its importance several times: 'nothing can have value, without being an object of utility. If the thing is useless, so is the labour contained in it',[2] and 'one of the first premises of selling was that a commodity should have use-value and should therefore satisfy a social need',[3] while demand and supply have, for him, the very definite function of explaining the fluctuations of prices around the equilibrium price, but not that of explaining the equilibrium price itself:[4] 'If supply and demand balance one another, they cease to explain anything, do not affect market values, and therefore leave us so much more in the dark about the reasons why the market value is expressed in just this sum of money and no other.'[5]

The labour theory of value fails on two different accounts. Firstly, it ignores the influence of demand on the scale of production, since prices may alter according to where a firm or enterprise chooses its point of output along its average cost curve. Unless constant costs predominate, costs will not be independent of output and will vary according to whether increasing or diminishing returns hold.[6] (The theory also avoids the problem of how to price goods which are produced in a multi-product firm or enjoy complementarities in production, but then similar problems arise in modern price theory as well.[7]) Secondly, it fails by omitting a very important element necessary to explain price formation, namely, the role played by scarce factors of production other than labour. It would hold true in Adam Smith's case of beaver and deer hunters, where labour is the only scarce factor and perfect mobility of resources

[1] Sweezy, *Capitalist Development*, p. 123.
[2] Marx, *Capital*, Vol. I, p. 41.   [3] Ibid. Vol. III, p. 178.
[4] E. Mandel, *Traité d'économie Marxiste*, Paris 1962, Vol. I, p. 193.
[5] Marx, *Capital*, Vol. III, p. 186.
[6] M. Dobb, *On Economic Theory and Socialism*, London 1955, p. 112.
[7] P. J. D. Wiles, *Price, Cost and Output*, Oxford 1956, p. 102.

between occupation is assured. It would also hold true if there
were only two homogeneous factors of production, labour and
capital, with uniform rates of wages and profits, perfect competition and uniform organic compositions of capital throughout
all branches of production, since then prices would all be pro-
portional to quantities of homogeneous labour used.[1] It could
in such a case be held as: 'a very special case' of neo-classical
price theory.[2] But when the first assumption is dropped and the
existence of non-homogeneous scarce natural resources, or of
types of labour that cannot be produced in unlimited amounts
by appropriate training, is admitted, then the labour theory of
value explanation of prices breaks down. By ignoring rents on
land or scarce natural resources and interest on capital, and by
contending that labour is the sole source of value, it automatically assumes that only labour is scarce, that other factors of
production, including capital, are 'gifts of nature' or products
of labour and that they have no part to play in price formation.
However, as long as the production of capital goods requires
refraining from consumption today, and thereby a limitation
on the level of consumption, any rational economic calculation
will have to utilize some rate of discount on future income (or
rate of interest to be included in the price of capital goods),
which will balance the desire for accrued income in the future
and the desire for consumption in the present (be this in the
eyes of individuals or in the preferences of the planners).
Without this, the demand for capital goods will always tend to
exceed the available supply, and decisions as to the correct rate
of investment, and as to the distribution of investment funds
between sectors, will be completely haphazard.[3] Once 'capital
accumulation has been carried on as far as to reduce the marginal *net* productivity of capital to zero, as a socialist society
would tend to do...interest charges are eliminated'.[4] Then
the labour theory of value may well be able to explain prices,
but before that stage its use in planning can only lead to serious
mistakes.

[1] H. D. Dickinson, notes to article by L. Johansen, 'Labour Theory of Value and
Marginal Utilities', *Economics of Planning*, Vol. III, No. 3, December 1963, p. 239.
[2] H. J. Sherman, 'Marxist Economics and Soviet Planning', *Soviet Studies*, Vol.
XVIII, No. 2, October 1966, p. 177.
[3] Dobb, *An Essay on Economic Growth and Planning*, London 1960, p. 87.
[4] Lange and Taylor, 'On the Economic Theory of Socialism', p. 133 (footnote 88).

It must not be forgotten, however, in criticizing Marx that, by adopting his theory of value, he was really following the tradition of the classical school of English political economy which had already affirmed that labour was at the basis of value.[1] Nor must it be forgotten that the theory was mainly used by him to explain certain features of the capitalist system through its reliance on the concept of 'surplus value', and was hardly meant to be an essay in price theory.[2] Just this fact could well have led to its being discarded, in the interest of greater economic rationality, by the socialist countries, who could have argued that it was only meant to apply to the capitalist system. This, however, was not done and the Soviet Union first, followed by the Eastern European countries later, clung to the Marxist categories of price and value, just when their rejection could have helped them to overcome many of the problems they were facing.[3] 'The lack of concern about rewards to factors other than labour, makes the theory of value particularly ill-adapted to the specific conditions of the communist economies. Indeed, it is a paradoxical whim of history that it should have been adopted as a frame of thinking in matters of practice precisely in that part of the world where waiting and abstinence is the central socioeconomic issue.'[4]

Whether in fact Marx did want 'value' to operate in the socialist economy is still a debated point. In the few references to the future socialist society given by Marx and Engels, both interpretations can be defended. In *Capital* Marx says: 'secondly, after the abolition of the capitalist mode of production, but still retaining social production, the determination of value continues to prevail in the sense that the regulation of labour-time and the distribution of social labour among the various production groups . . . becomes more essential than ever',[5] while

[1] R. L. Meek, *Studies in the Labour Theory of Value*, London 1956.
[2] J. Robinson, *An Essay on Marxian Economics*, London 1947.
[3] It is only recently that more liberal economists have argued that the proper field for Marxist theories should be that of income distribution and macro-economic development, while the technical questions of resource allocation may best be discussed in terms of western economics; see Sherman, 'Marxist Economics', p. 181; J. Goldmann and J. Flek, 'Economic Growth in Czechoslovakia', *Economics of Planning*, Vol. vi, No. 2, 1966, p. 127.
[4] A. Zauberman, 'The Soviet Debate on the Law of Value and Price Formation', in G. Grossman (ed.), *Value and Plan*, Berkeley and Los Angeles 1960, p. 21.
[5] Marx, *Capital*, Vol. iii, p. 830.

Engels argues that 'society will not assign values to products'[1] and 'people will be able to manage everything very simply, without the intervention of much-vaunted "value"'.[2] A good deal of the confusion may, in fact, be due to different definitions of the society of the future. It would seem that in the utopia of a fully communist society commodity production, and hence value, will disappear.[3] This will be the age of: 'From each according to his ability, to each according to his needs.'[4] But in the transition period between capitalism and communism, economic accounting and value still appear.[5] In fact, the existence of value as an economic category in the Soviet Union has been reaffirmed countless times by Russian economists in their discussions on the operation of the 'Law of Value' in the U.S.S.R. This discussion, too, has not always been altogether clear and straightforward, as witnessed by the remark of a Polish economist: 'In hardly any other theoretical problem has confusion reached similar dimensions.'[6] As to the existence of the 'Law of Value' in the Soviet Union, by now most people agree that it operates, following the two path-breaking statements made just after the war.[7] Whether this is because a private (in fact, co-operative) sector exists side by side with a public one, as was stated by Stalin,[8] or because, as a Western Marxist economist holds, the Soviet Union has not yet reached socialism,[9] is immaterial. The conclusion is by now widely accepted: the 'Law of Value', though modified by planning, operates in the Soviet Union.

But the 'Law of Value' and value itself must not be confused. The 'Law of Value' is a general equilibrium theory[10] which 'summarizes those forces at work in a commodity-

[1] Engels, *Anti-Dühring*, p. 426.   [2] Ibid, p. 427.

[3] Marx, *Critique of the Gotha Programme*, p. 31.

[4] Ibid.   [5] Ibid. pp. 29–31.

[6] W. Brus, 'The Law of Value and the Market Mechanism in a Socialist Economy', in *Problems of Economic Theory and Practice in Poland—Studies on the Theory of Reproduction and Prices*, Warsaw 1964, p. 301.

[7] Anonymous, 'Teaching of Economics in the Soviet Union', translated from the Russian (*Pod Znamenem Marxisma*, No. 7–8, 1943) in *The American Economic Review*, Vol. xxxiv, No. 3, September 1944; J. Stalin, *Economic Problems of Socialism in the U.S.S.R.*, Moscow 1952, p. 23.

[8] Stalin, *Economic Problems of Socialism in the U.S.S.R.*, pp. 19–21.

[9] Mandel, *Traité d'économie Marxiste*, Vol. II, pp. 426–7.

[10] O. Lange, 'Marxian Economics and Modern Economic Theory', *The Review of Economic Studies*, Vol. II, No. 3, June 1935, p. 194.

producing society which regulate (*a*) the exchange ratios among commodities, (*b*) the quantity of each produced, and (*c*) the allocation of the labor force to the various branches of production'.[1] Value is only the expression of the labour socially necessary to produce a commodity. Though there is no necessary link between the two, they have often been bundled together, as in a much-quoted Soviet source: 'Utilizing the law of value, the Soviet state sets as its goal the establishment of commodity prices based on the socially-necessary costs of their production.'[2] Marxist value therefore lies at the basis of Soviet prices, even though allowance is made for some deviations. This has been repeatedly reaffirmed by most Russian economists who, though having had different views on price formation, have all paid homage to Marx's basic theory.[3] One author, for instance, states that 'at the basis of price formation in all sectors of production must lie one and the same principle: the price must reflect the social expenditure of live and congealed labour on the production of this or that item of production'.[4] Another affirms that: 'price is the expression of value, [and] in the conditions of a socialist economy...the law of value is also the law of prices, that is, the law regulating prices';[5] and Nemchinov, one of the best-known Soviet economists, also threw his authoritative weight behind the view that price and value are linked under socialism.[6] All this does not mean, however, that prices in Eastern Europe faithfully reflect the labour theory of value, since many other influences, apart from fidelity to Marx, enter into their formation.

Whether, in any case, values can be calculated at all in a socialist economy is still an open question. Engels thought that this would be extremely easy: 'From the moment when society enters into possession of the means of production...the quantity of labour contained in a product need not...be established

[1] Sweezy, *Capitalist Development*, pp. 52–3.
[2] Anonymous, 'Teaching of Economics', p. 523.
[3] M. Bornstein, 'The Soviet Price Reform Discussion', *The Quarterly Journal of Economics*, Vol. LXXVIII, No. 1, February 1964, p. 24.
[4] I. Malyshev, 'Nekotorye voprosy tsenoobrazovanya v sotsialisticheskom khozyaistve', *Voprosy Ekonomiki*, No. 3, March 1957, p. 93.
[5] Y. A. Kronrod, 'Stoimost kak basa tseni v uslovyach sotsialisticheskoi ekonomiki', *Voprosy Ekonomiki*, No. 10, October 1960, p. 84.
[6] V. Nemchinov, 'Stoimost i tsena pri sotsialisme', *Voprosy Ekonomiki*, No. 12, December 1960, p. 88.

in a roundabout way... Society can simply calculate how many hours of labour are contained in a steam-engine';[1] but since then opinions have been less optimistic. Some Soviet and non-Soviet economists think that it will be impossible to calculate socially necessary labour times.[2] Others, however, hold that labour values can be obtained by solution of an optimum plan[3] or of an input–output table.[4] It is true that, thanks to the latter approach, it has now become possible to measure all direct and indirect labour inputs, expressed in man-years per physical or value output, so that a price system based on labour values is now feasible.[5] Such a price formation procedure, though distorted by the initial defects of the labour theory of value, could well be more meaningful than the present ones, based on prices that are, more or less, irrational.[6]

Foreign trade and labour values

Applying the labour theory of value to the international sphere creates a whole array of new problems. The question of whether the law of value operates is again a subject of confusion. According to some Western authors it does not,[7] according to most Eastern ones it does, though its working is modified.[8] But given,

---

[1] Engels, *Anti-Dühring*, p. 426.

[2] K. Gatovski, 'Ob ispol'sovanyi zakona stoimosti v sostialisticheskom khozyaistve', *Kommunist*, No. 9, June 1957, p. 47.

[3] Nemchinov, 'Stoimost i tsena', pp. 99–103; W. Brus and K. Laski, 'The Law of Value and the Problem of Allocation in Socialism', in *On Political Economy and Econometrics—Essays in honour of Oskar Lange*, Warsaw 1964, pp. 47–8.

[4] O. Bogomolov (ed.), *Ekonomicheskaya effektivnost mezhdunarodnogo sotsialisticheskogo rasdelenie truda*, Moscow 1965, p. 69.

[5] A. Zauberman, 'A note on the Soviet Inter-Industry Labour Input Balance', *Soviet Studies*, Vol. xv, No. 1, July 1963, p. 53.

[6] The possibility of obtaining a consistent price system based on labour inputs has created the further possibility of deducting values from prices. Instead of the usual problem, which was that of deriving prices from values, an 'inverse transformation problem' can now be posed. Solution of the latter would provide 'some objective (i.e. non-arbitrary) and consistent basis for attaching relative weights to heterogeneous products', M. Morishima and F. Seton, 'Aggregation in Leontief Matrices and the Labour Theory of Value', *Econometrica*, Vol. xxix, No. 2, April 1961, p. 203.

[7] Sweezy, *Capitalist Development*, p. 289; J. Schumpeter, *History of Economic Analysis*, London 1955, p. 612.

[8] G. Kohlmey, *Der demokratische Weltmarkt*, Berlin 1956, p. 206; V. Cerniansky, 'Die Preisbasis auf dem sozialistischen Weltmarkt', *Der Aussenhandel*, Nos. 4–5, March 1958, p. 153; J. Mervart, 'The Significance of certain Problems of the

from the previous analysis, that a socialist country will try to price its goods on the basis of labour value, whether or not the law of value holds, the answer will not influence the criteria on which its (planned) foreign trade policy is based. Two main cases arise from the point of view of international trade: (a) the case of exchanges between one socialist country (or group of countries) and the rest of the world, presumed to remain capitalist, and (b) the case of exchanges among socialist countries, all of them relying on the labour theory of value.

The first case is quite straightforward. The country in question will consider the domestic cost (i.e. value) in social labour of every commodity and compare it with the foreign currency price it could fetch on the world market. Those lines of production which give the country the biggest possible returns in international purchasing power in return for a given outlay of social labour will be developed for export purposes, and vice versa for imports (apart from any political or other economic reservations which could run against such a straight-forward comparative advantage method).[1] This seems, in fact, the practice at present followed by most Eastern European countries, with the qualification that in their comparisons with world prices they do not use pure values, but either a distorted price or some estimate of production cost which reflects labour values only imperfectly.[2] The more interesting case is that which arises out of exchanges between socialist countries. The problem here is of finding some common basis for international values and, in the light of this, working out foreign trade criteria. Following Marx, international value is not determined by any average of national values, but by the socially necessary labour time and the social conditions of production in the countries which supply the bulk of any particular commodity on the world market.[3] Thus: 'the determining factor in the planned price formation will have to be the international value

Operation of the Law of Value on the World Socialist Market', *Czechoslovak Economic Papers*, No. 1, Prague 1959.
[1] Ch. Bettelheim, *Studies in the Theory of Planning*, Asia Publishing House, 1959, pp. 257–8.
[2] See Chapter 5.
[3] M. Horovitz, 'A propos de certaines particularités et de certaines limitations de la Loi de la Valeur dans le commerce extérieur socialiste', translated from the Rumanian (*Probleme Economice*, No. 4, 1958) in *Etudes Economiques*, Nos. 112–13, 1958, p. 82.

of commodities reflecting socially necessary expenditures...on the world market, and not the national values of production of commodities in the separate countries'.[1] That the problems of finding such a price system are very great is admitted,[2] but in theory at least the possibility of rational foreign trade calculations on the basis of the labour theory of value can be vindicated. In fact, several authors use values, reflecting socially necessary labour times, to show the advantages accruing to socialist countries from foreign trade.[3]

The use of such a system does, however, create a serious problem which has been admitted by Eastern European economists, i.e. the problem of exploitation.[4] According to Marx, an exchange is equivalent if two products contain the same amounts of labour time.[5] But in such a case exchange on the world market will be, almost automatically, non-equivalent, since a country in which productive conditions are more developed will be able to produce given values in a shorter labour time than others and will, therefore, be able to 'sell its goods above their value even though cheaper than the competing countries...The favoured country recovers more labour in exchange for less labour.'[6] Thus: 'two countries can exchange between themselves...so that both of them will gain, but in any case there will always be one which will gain a greater advantage (übervorteilt wird)'.[7] If this is the case, equivalent exchanges on the basis of the labour theory of value are not possible and within the socialist world market itself exploitation of the less developed by the more industrial countries will be inevitable. A way out has, however, been provided. It is argued that, on the international scale, given the different intensities (i.e.

[1] I. Aizenberg, 'Ekonomicheskye predposilki povishenya roli Rublya v mezhdunarodnich rastchetach', *Dengi i Kredit*, No. 4, April 1962, p. 34.
[2] I. Dudinskii, 'Nekotorye tcherti rasvitya mirovogo sotsialisticheskogo rinka', *Voprosy Ekonomiki*, No. 2, February 1961, p. 45.
[3] Cerniansky, 'Problems of the Economic Efficiency of Foreign Trade', *Czechoslovak Economic Papers*, No. 1, Prague 1959, pp. 115–16; Mervart, 'Problems of Operation of Law of Value', pp. 92–6.
[4] O. Bogomolov, 'Metodologitcheskye problemi mezhdunarodonogo sotsialistischeskogo rasdelenya truda', *Voprosy Ekonomiki*, No. 11, November 1963, p. 11; I. Vajda, 'Probleme und Formen der Wirtschaftskooperation der sozialistischen Länder', *Wirtschaftswissenschaft*, No. 10, October 1964, p. 1658.
[5] Marx, *A Contribution to the Critique of Political Economy*, 2nd edition, Chicago 1913, p. 28. [6] Marx, *Capital*, Vol. III, pp. 232–3.
[7] Marx, *Gründrisse der Kritik der Politischen Ökonomie*, Berlin 1953, p. 755.

productivities) of labour in the various countries, the concept of equivalent exchange postulated by Marx for a closed economy is incorrect.[1] (In fact, it would rule out specialization based on comparative—as opposed to absolute—advantage. The England of Ricardo's example would never be able to sell anything to Portugal since the work of 100 men per year produces consistently more in Portugal than in England in both lines of activity.) The way to achieve an equivalent exchange is by having such an international division of labour that each country, through international trade, though it exchanges different quantities of labour time, achieves the *same saving* in labour time: 'The equality of exchange does not mean that an equal quantity of labour time is contained in the exchanged goods but it means that as a result of the exchange both the partners receive an *equal gain*.'[2]

Theoretically, therefore, one can have a price system which both reflects labour times and does not lead to unequal exchange. This would seem to be the system towards which CMEA should tend, given the often-expressed desire to abandon the use of world prices and to switch over to an independent price system. It is rather doubtful whether much of the present volume of intra-CMEA trade would conform to the rather stringent requirements of equivalent exchange but, none the less, if one is to believe official pronouncements: 'It is necessary continually to perfect the system of price formation on the world socialist market...while creating conditions for the gradual change-over to an independent price basis.'[3] But international prices based on labour times are not very easily defendable on theoretical grounds, nor do they seem to be much desired in practice, even though occasional lip service is paid to them. Given the shortcomings of the labour theory of value, these would only be transplanted onto an international scale. The lack of interest rate calculation and the consequent undervaluation of capital-intensive goods would lead to the demand for imports of such goods constantly outstripping their supply. Since demand and supply cannot, according to Marx's

---

[1] Mervart, 'Problems of Operation of Law of Value', p. 104.

[2] L. B. Shaynin, 'Proportions of Exchange', *The Economic Journal*, Vol. LXX, No. 280, December 1960, p. 772.

[3] CMEA, *Basic Principles of International Socialist Division of Labour*, Section 7, quoted in: M. C. Kaser, *Comecon*, 2nd edition, London 1967, p. 254.

analysis, by themselves bring about a permanent deviation of price from value, the logical outcome of relying only on the labour theory of value would be to encourage countries to specialize in those lines of production which, from an international point of view, are more profitable, i.e. labour-intensive ones. That this course has not so far been followed by Eastern European countries is amply shown by their recent economic history.

A further criticism which could be levelled at a labour theory of value price system is that, like traditional comparative advantage theory, it is of a static nature and cannot predict, unless accompanied by conscious international planning, which will be the most profitable future patterns of specialization in each country. In any case, though it is possible to calculate labour times within a country, it would be much more difficult to calculate socially necessary labour times on the international sphere.[1]

Eastern European practice

As far as is known, only one Eastern European country has ever seriously proposed to adopt labour time as the basis for independent prices. This country is Bulgaria, which seems to have the lowest labour productivity in industry within CMEA,[2] and would stand to gain most from such a switch since 'such a price basis would give those with low productivity favourable terms of trade, for man-hour pricing would ensure good prices for their exports and they would pay relatively low prices for the capital-intensive products they import'.[3] Such a policy would, however, lead to rather different results according to whether absolute or partial specialization were to be achieved. If Bulgaria were the only producer of a commodity and could sell it at a price dictated by its labour inputs, the terms of trade would move in its favour vis-à-vis countries that produce other commodities in more capital-intensive ways. But then it could achieve such a gain with any form of pricing, simply by using its monopoly power. If, on the other hand, Bulgaria were to be

---

[1] Cerniansky, 'Problems of the Economic Efficiency of Foreign Trade', p. 119; Mervart, 'Problems of Operation of Law of Value', p. 92.

[2] Kaser, *Comecon*, p. 196.

[3] Ibid. p. 197.

only one of several suppliers of the commodity in question, the more productive countries would either be able to enjoy a large 'producers' surplus' if prices were pegged at the Bulgarian level, or more probably, would attempt to sell at a lower price and therefore undercut Bulgaria. In fact, given that Bulgaria has a lower level of productivity than the other countries, it will always use more labour per unit of output and will, therefore, be the highest cost supplier of the area. Aligning intra-CMEA prices on Bulgarian labour costs could only lead to a marked reduction of international trade, if prices were to be strictly enforced, or to competitive bidding by other countries, if some latitude was given to trade negotiators.

In any case, Czech and East German economists have rejected the idea of labour values for international trade pricing and have argued either, subtly, in favour of a unique price system for capitalist and socialist countries alike, which would clearly not be based on labour values:

The more the prices on the socialist world market conform to international ones, the better will they serve the development of exchanges and the growth of production.[1]

and:

This process [growth] would be retarded by keeping up the present system of fixing prices for the world socialist market, as it is unscientific, supports conservatism and the scattering of resources, protects artificially technical backwardness and impedes the growth of the productivity of social labour.[2]

or, more openly:

The adoption of national labour outlays as trade prices between CMEA members as a principle would make more difficult mutual advantage in goods exchange and would hinder the achievement of a rational international division of labour.[3]

Since the labour theory of value does not appear to be the

[1] Cerniansky, 'Die Preisbasis auf dem sozialistischen Weltmarkt', p. 153.
[2] V. Kaigl, 'International Division of Labour in the World Socialist System', *Czechoslovak Economic Papers*, No. 1, Prague 1959, p. 18.
[3] W. Maier and H. Mann, 'Die Grosshandelspreise als Ausgangspunkt für die Schaffung einer eigenen Preisbasis im Handel zwischen den sozialistischen Ländern', *Wirtschaftswissenschaft*, No. 4, April 1964, p. 601.

answer to the problem of finding an independent intra-socialist price system, a few other solutions have been suggested. Physical indicators could provide some guide as to comparative advantage (indices, that is, comparing the physical productivity of labour per man-hour, or the quantity of raw materials used up per unit of output, etc.),[1] and it seems that research on such indicators is going on at present within CMEA, though their use must be limited to few, relatively homogeneous lines of production.[2] A DDR economist has argued that, with time, the prices of CMEA trade would approximate more and more closely to those of the Soviet Union,[3] but no economic justification whatsoever is given for such a tendency and it has been attacked within Eastern Europe itself: 'it is evident that...the national value of one country cannot become a basis of international exchange'.[4] As for Yugoslavia, when it accused the Soviet Union of exploitation in international trade, it suggested the use of some kind of 'special prices' which, it was argued, it had used in trade with Albania before 1948.[5] These prices took into account 'the real situation of Albanian economy...as the starting point',[6] so that 'the economically more developed Yugoslavia did not extract any extra profits from Albania'.[7] But the basis on which these 'special prices' should be fixed is left totally unclear. They should probably be 'some ad-hoc prices adjusted to take account of the larger "labour content"

[1] Mervart, 'Problems of Operation of Law of Value', p. 97.
[2] Bogomolov, 'Mezhdunarodnoe sotsialistitcheskoe rasdelenya truda', *Voprosy Ekonomiki*, No. 1, January 1960, p. 17.
[3] Kohlmey, *Demokratische Weltmarkt*, p. 267.
[4] Mervart, 'Problems of Operation of Law of Value', p. 99. Theoretically, of course, it is possible that the prices used internally in one country could also be used in trade with other countries. This case arises when the country whose prices are used is so much larger than its partner, or partners, that the latter can exert no pressure on the former's supply and demand schedules by trading with it. In such a case, which is however of possible application only for a restricted number of commodities, all the gains from trade are reaped by the smaller countries and no benefits at all go to the larger one; C. P. Kindleberger: *International Economics*, revised edition, Homewood, Ill. 1958, pp. 88–91. In the Eastern European situation the Soviet Union would be the obvious candidate for such a position, though of course its weight is very great only in the case of some primary products. What is surprising is that criticism of such a view should have been voiced in a smaller Eastern European country, which would have benefited from such special conditions of exchange.
[5] M. Popovic, *On Economic Relations among Socialist Countries*, London 1950, p. 49.
[6] Ibid.
[7] Ibid.

of the exports of the less-developed countries of the area';[1]
though, according to P. Wiles, they were not just *ad hoc*, but
actually based on chance.[2]

All that remains, therefore, is reliance on world market
prices, in so far as these can be ascertained. Though 'monopolies, trade cycles, inflations due to military pressures, etc...'
are at work on the capitalist markets and, therefore, distort
prices from their values, none the less a Marxist justification of
their use has been given: 'It is held that these prices [i.e. world
prices] have been formed by a long historical process and reflect,
in last analysis, the international value of commodities.'[3] In any
case, some of the price fluctuations which take place on the
world market are cushioned off by the practice of holding prices
in intra-CMEA trade steady for relatively long periods of time.
The economic justification for their use sounds much more
plausible. It is based on the contention that, should CMEA
prices deviate for any length of time from world prices, if the
socialist price was higher every country would be induced to
purchase the commodity in question from capitalist suppliers
while, should the socialist price be lower no country would have
any incentive to sell within the bloc.[4] The argument can, however, be disputed. Though, *prima facie*, it would seem that
unhampered world prices are the most rational system for
CMEA, since they can be considered as opportunity cost prices,
this only holds true if trade between CMEA and the rest of the
world is completely free and specialization optimal. Since this
is far from being the case, it can be argued that for commodities in which the area is self-sufficient, an intra-CMEA
price system could be more suitable. Such a system would take
into account not the world's scarcity relations, but those
prevailing within the area. The present case of raw material
production can be used as an apt illustration. The recent move
to 1960–4 world prices in intra-CMEA trade has moved the
terms of trade against primary products and has aggravated the
already existing problem of overproduction of machinery and

[1] N. Spulber, 'The Dispute: Economic Relations among Socialist States and the
Soviet "Model"', in V. L. Benes, R. F. Byrnes, N. Spulber (eds.), *The Second
Soviet–Yugoslav Dispute*, Indiana University 1959, p. xxxvi.
[2] Wiles, *Communist International Economics*, Oxford 1968, p. 18.
[3] Horovitz, 'A propos de certaines particularités', p. 88.
[4] Cerniansky, 'Die Preisbasis auf dem sozialistischen Weltmarkt', p. 153.

scarcity of raw materials.[1] To encourage raw material production an elaborate system of mutual credits has therefore been
envisaged and is being partly applied. It would have been
simpler not to alter the previous price structure or even to
improve the terms of trade of the raw material producing
countries, despite the movement of world prices. But present
tendencies seem to favour the continuing use of world prices
while the creation of an intra-CMEA price system is being
relegated to the distant future.[2]

From all this one can draw the conclusion that the Marxist
category of value, as the socially necessary labour time needed
to produce a commodity, is disappearing from economic practice both within the communist countries and in their mutual
external relations. Already a whole school of thought in the
Soviet Union, though still phrasing its arguments in Marxist
terms, is trying to set up price formation methods that take into
account the scarcity of capital goods and natural resources.[3]
In Poland socially necessary labour time has been defined as
including some element of interest and as being based on
marginal costs,[4] while differential rent has been officially
accepted in the USSR.[5] As a Polish economist has put it:

There is no reason to consider interest differently from, for example,
commodities, money, profit, etc. which are linked to commodity
production and which manifest themselves in the socialist economy,
even if there they show different social-economic characteristics
than in capitalism. In socialism a part of what is produced for
society takes the form of interest, which is not, therefore, any more
a part of surplus value, i.e. one of the categories of exploitation. But
interest in itself can and does exist even today in the field of short-
term credits, and no one considers this as a violation of the principles
of a socialist economy.[6]

This may well be an obituary on the price formation practices
so far used in Eastern Europe. In fact, ideology (or better, the

---

[1] United Nations, Economic Commission for Europe, *Economic Survey of Europe in
1966*, New York 1967, Ch. 3, p. 2.

[2] G. Kohlmey, 'Karl Marx' Theorie von den internationalen Werten', *Probleme
der Politischen Ökonomie*, Berlin 1962, pp. 82–3.

[3] Bornstein, 'Soviet Price Reform Discussion', pp. 36–45.

[4] Brus and Laski, 'Law of Value and Problem of Allocation in Socialism', p. 45.

[5] Zauberman, 'The Soviet Debate on the Law of Value', pp. 21–2.

[6] Brus, 'Sul ruolo della legge del valore nell'Economia socialista', in *Vecchia e
Nuova Pianificazione Economica in Polonia*, Milan 1960, pp. 50–1.

distorted view of Marxism considered as ideology in the Soviet bloc) will not dictate its methods to economic policy beyond a certain point. A French student of the influence of Marxism in the Soviet Union argued that 'Soviet ideology is an instrument of the politics of the Party and the State',[1] and an American concluded that 'although the Marxian ideology has exerted some influence (in part, harmful) on the economy, the main role of ideology has been to justify and legitimize the strategy and tactics of Soviet economic development'.[2] The labour theory of value is probably a case in point. For a time it was used as a major proof of fidelity to Marxism. Internally it is now becoming a fetter, and is being discarded in favour of economically more rational price policies. Internationally it never saw the light, and its future implementation in the world socialist market is becoming more and more unlikely.[3]

[1] H. Chambre, *Le Marxisme en Union Soviétique*, Paris 1955, pp. 506–8.
[2] Bornstein, 'Ideology and the Soviet Economy', *Soviet Studies*, Vol. xviii, No. 1, July 1966, p. 74.
[3] Mervart, *Vyznam a vyvojcem v mezinarodnim obchode* (English summary), Prague 1960, p. 282.

2

THE LANGE–LERNER SOLUTION

Marx's analysis of the future socialist state was never outlined in any detail, his main preoccupation having been the examination of the existing capitalist system. Though some of his later followers attempted a more comprehensive analysis of the economics of socialism, it was left, ironically enough, to Barone and Pareto, who can hardly be said to be in the Marxist tradition, to set out a blueprint for a planned economy.[1] Their very centralized solution, which they themselves considered impracticable, was later elaborated, mainly by O. Lange and A. P. Lerner, who, in the framework of Western economic theory, transformed it into a highly decentralized system, with a much better chance of implementation.[2] Their solution is usually referred to as the 'Lange–Lerner' model.

The main characteristic of this model is the adaptation of the perfectly competitive market system of a capitalist economy to the needs of a centrally planned one. In the Lange–Lerner scheme all industry is state-owned. Nevertheless the managers of enterprises behave as profit-maximizing entrepreneurs under perfect competition, equating given prices with marginal costs, while the managers of whole industries attempt to minimize their industries' average costs. The prices may be market prices determined by demand and supply, in the case of consumer goods, or accounting or shadow prices fixed by the central planning board, in the case of capital goods. The main point

---

[1] V. Pareto, *Cours d'Economie Politique*, Nouvelle édition, Paris 1964, Tome II, pp. 90–4, 364–71; E. Barone, 'The Ministry of Production in the Collectivist State', translated from the Italian (*Giornale degli Economisti e Rivista di Statistica*, September–October 1908), in F. A. von Hayek (ed.), *Collectivist Economic Planning*, London 1938.

[2] O. Lange and F. M. Taylor, 'On the Economic Theory of Socialism', in B. E. Lippincott (ed.), *On the Economic Theory of Socialism*, University of Minnesota 1938; A. P. Lerner, 'Economic Theory and Socialist Economy', *The Review of Economic Studies*, Vol. II, No. 1, October 1934; 'A Note on Socialist Economics', *The Review of Economic Studies*, Vol. IV, No. 1, October 1936; 'Statics and Dynamics in Socialist Economics', *The Economic Journal*, Vol. XLVII, No. 186, June 1937; *The Economics of Control*, New York 1944.

is that their 'parametric function' is maintained. Under capitalism this function is assured by the fact that 'although the prices are a resultant of the behaviour of all individuals on the market, each individual separately regards the actual market prices as given data to which he has to adjust himself'.[1] Under socialism prices will maintain this function—those for consumer goods will be determined by the market, those of capital goods will be fixed by the planning board so as to equilibrate demand and supply by a trial-and-error procedure —and will, therefore, be outside the control of individual managers.

Given, thus, that prices maintain their function as parameters, and that managers are subject to certain rules as to inputs, outputs and pricing, the substitution of a planning board for a competitive market is feasible and can lead to optimum resource allocation. It was also argued that the scheme was in practice the only one likely to lead to perfect resource allocation and was not merely feasible but also desirable. The argument was based on the imperfections existing in the capitalist world (for instance, monopolistic competition or oligopolies), which make perfect resource allocation an unattainable ideal. The socialist blueprint would avoid these distortions by central action. The welfare skeleton of pure competitive theory was shown not to be incompatible with socialist institutions and collective ownership. On the contrary, the latter were probably the best means to attain the ideals of the theory created by the supporters of 'laissez-faire'.[2]

Applications to foreign trade

Hardly anything was said, however, on the foreign trade problems of such an economy.[3] Lange never mentions them; Lerner refers to them, but not in detail, in *The Economics of Control*. His main point is that the managers of importing agencies will import goods from abroad up to 'the point where a

---

[1] Lange and Taylor, 'Economic Theory of Socialism', p. 70.

[2] I. M. D. Little, *A Critique of Welfare Economics*, Second Edition, Oxford 1960, pp. 260–1.

[3] G. Haberler, 'Theoretical Reflections on the Trade of Socialist Economies', in A. A. Brown and E. Neuberger (eds.), *International Trade and Central Planning*, Berkeley and Los Angeles 1968, pp. 30–1.

domestic dollar's worth of foreign currency can purchase an amount of foreign goods that can be sold at home for a dollar',[1] and vice versa for exporting agencies. Thus, assuming no discrimination between domestic and foreign goods, 'the prices of foreign commodities will perform a function similar to that of prices fixed by the planning board'.[2] Managers would consider these prices as given, just like all other home prices, and would purchase those factors or commodities which they could obtain more cheaply, whether foreign or domestic. In fact, the presence or absence of foreign trade state agencies would seem irrelevant. As for the rate of exchange, it could be considered as another accounting price, whose level would be set so as to equilibrate the demand and supply of foreign currency. In other words, abstracting from transport costs, complete specialization, tariffs or other restrictions on trade, foreign trade would be carried on until the relative prices of goods were equalized at home and abroad. The criteria by which to choose the country's exports or imports are, therefore, relatively simple. Comparative costs provide the answer, just as in a capitalist world. Whether state trading agencies or individual managers decide on the choice of volume of exports and imports, the criteria underlying these decisions remain the same. Another writer on the subject confirms this point: 'The principle of comparative costs applies to a socialist economy as to a capitalist one.'[3]

In general, therefore, the foreign trade side of such a 'competitive' socialist economy falls again within the pattern of static welfare theory. Foreign trade will be carried on until relative prices are equal in the world as a whole and welfare will be maximized, either in the Paretian sense that more can be obtained of one good without anything having to be given up of the other (in Figure 1, a country would reach such an optimum if it were to trade along the international price-line TT, producing at P' and moving to any consumption point between points A and B, its pre-trade production and consumption point having been at P), or else in the sense that the country

---

[1] Lerner, *The Economics of Control*, p. 346.
[2] B. F. Hoselitz, 'Socialist Planning and International Economic Relations', *The American Economic Review*, Vol. xxxiii, No. 4, December 1943, p. 173.
[3] H. D. Dickinson, *Economics of Socialism*, Oxford 1939, p. 173.

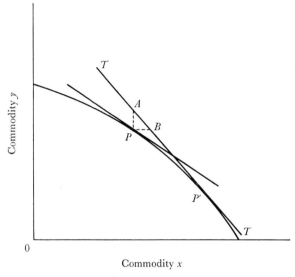

FIGURE I

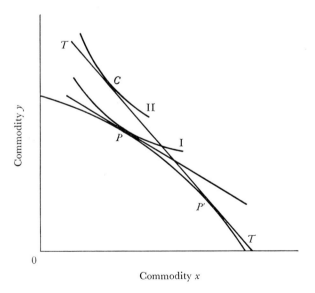

FIGURE 2

moves upwards on its community indifference-curve structure, even though it is now consuming less than before of one of the two goods. (In Figure 2 the country, by trading along the internation price-line TT, reaches point C on the higher indifference curve II; it will now be consuming fewer units of the good it enjoys a comparative advantage in, but more of the good it imports, than in the pre-trade position.) In the case of the socialist economy, some of the difficulties associated with the use of community indifference curves can be overlooked if we suppose that the planning board itself fixes the country's preference scale. Presumably, while the criterion for choosing an export or an import would be based on price differentials, the underlying reason would be factor endowment differences as outlined by the Heckscher–Ohlin model.[1] Thus exports would tend to be concentrated in those industries in which the relatively abundant factor in the socialist economy was intensive, and vice versa for imports.

It would seem that little more need be said on the subject of foreign trade criteria in the Lange–Lerner scheme. The criteria by which the structure of imports and exports is decided in the capitalist world are directly translated into the new framework. No conceptual differences exist; only the organizational set-up needs to be altered. Dickinson lists a few exceptions to the comparative advantage principle (political reasons for not being too dependent on some foreign country, social reasons for developing some branch beyond the level dictated by comparative advantage),[2] but these do not amount to any newly found purely economic criteria that would do away with the theory of comparative costs. There is a field, however, in which the Lange–Lerner economy may be better suited to apply another foreign trade criterion originally developed for market economies, and that is the field of infant industries. Here the main argument rests on the possibility of a divergence between private and social costs in some line of production. If private costs only are taken into consideration, the country could be led into a 'wrong' pattern of international specialization. In

[1] E. Heckscher, 'The Effect of Foreign Trade on the Distribution of Income', translated from the Swedish (*Ekonomisk Tidskrift*, Vol. XXI, 1919), in The American Economic Association, *Readings in the Theory of International Trade*, London 1950.
[2] Dickinson, *Economics of Socialism*, pp. 175–6.

Figure 3 it is assumed that a country can produce good y under conditions of increasing, and good x under conditions of decreasing costs. If the international price ratio is shown by the line TT (and $T'T'$), then production will take place at P' and consumption at C. This is an inferior point to the pre-trade one

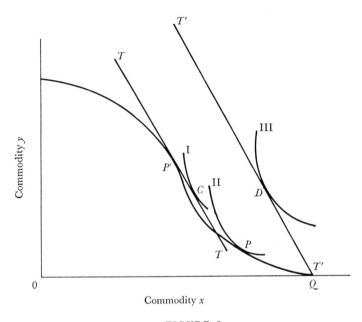

FIGURE 3

of P. If, however, there was knowledge of the possibility of increasing returns in good x, then production would be shifted to point Q (and consumption to the much more advantageous point D), and the country in question would invert its previous specialization pattern.[1]

Lange argues that a socialist economy would be better placed to take into account such divergences between private and social costs: 'A socialist economy would be able to put *all* the alternatives into its economic accounting. Thus it would evaluate *all* the services rendered by production and take into the cost

[1] J. Tinbergen, *International Economic Co-operation*, Amsterdam 1945, Appendix 1; R. E. Caves, *Trade and Economic Structure*, Cambridge, Mass. 1960, pp. 171–2.

accounts *all* the alternatives sacrificed.'[1] And, more specifically
for the case under consideration: 'A very important case of
benefits and costs which the private producer cannot consider
arises when external economies or diseconomies of scale are
present.'[2] In this field it would seem, therefore, that some kind
of definite criteria for foreign trade could be found, provided
the evidence of external economies for infant industries was
present. Within a static framework such evidence may not be
forthcoming. For the case to be valid, the economies should be
external to the firm (otherwise output would be expanded
automatically and there would be no need for protection), and
internal to the industry. Since the concomitance of both these
conditions seems rather unlikely, Viner came to the conclusion
that the whole case was of the nature of a 'theoretical curiosity'.[3]
This, however, is to ignore the broader structural and dynamic
problems in the less-developed countries for which the argument
was originally developed.[4]

Consideration of underdeveloped countries leads one to
several other cases that can be made against the adoption of a
specialization pattern based on comparative advantage, which
could lead to increasing reliance on exports of primary products
or to a shift of resources into an agricultural sector already
plagued by under-employed labour. But it is doubtful how far
one could apply a Lange–Lerner model to such an economy,
which is usually bedevilled by distortions and lacks the competitive commodity and factor markets and the rather sophisticated production mechanisms which would seem to be essential
to the model's functioning. All the other arguments for protection
are not really trade criteria arguments. The well-known optimum tariff theory is applicable to the Lange–Lerner economy
just as to any non-socialist country.[5] As for the income distribution effects of tariffs,[6] these are better attained by direct
changes in the social dividend (one of the categories of remunera-

[1] Lange and Taylor, 'Economic Theory of Socialism', p. 104.
[2] Ibid. p. 105.
[3] J. Viner, *Studies in the Theory of International Trade*, London 1937, p. 481.
[4] H. Myint, 'Infant Industry Arguments for Assistance to Industries in the Setting
of Dynamic Trade Theory' in R. Harrod and D. Hague (eds.), *International Trade
Theory in a Developing World*, London 1963, pp. 174–5.
[5] Little, *Critique of Welfare Economics*, p. 253.
[6] W. F. Stolper and P. A. Samuelson, 'Protection and Real Wages', *The Review
of Economic Studies*, Vol. IX, November 1941.

tion directly in the hands of the Lange–Lerner state) going to different factors of production, rather than by tariffs on certain goods (which always carry with them the danger of retaliation).

One can see, therefore, that the general body of international trade and welfare theory is transplanted into the model. The static nature of both of these is maintained, almost *in toto*, and few of those changes normally assumed to be of a socialist nature are introduced, at least within the realm of economics. There seems to be no conscious will to alter the plans for production and trade in a growth-maximizing direction. The central board only fixes the total amount to be invested in a period, while the direction and form of the investment are left to the atomistic decisions taken by managers, who are, in all likelihood, ignorant of each others' plans.[1] As Sweezy states: 'Lange's board is not a planning agency at all but rather a price-fixing agency.'[2] In the field of foreign trade, with the exception of the external economies argument, there is no attempt to criticize the static nature of the comparative advantage theory and the risks involved in blindly following the specialization pattern it prescribes at any moment of time.[3] While in purely theoretical terms the model is feasible, and also leads to optimum resource allocation, in practical terms it would have to be quite seriously modified to take into account the problems of changes and growth in factor endowment through development and trade itself. The whole question of alternative growth patterns brought about by different trade and specialization patterns, a problem facing both the underdeveloped world and the Soviet area, is ignored. A coherent and tightly knit set of theoretical assumptions and considerations can be found in the Lange–Lerner model, but its applied significance seems to be, and has so far been, rather limited.

The Lange–Lerner model and present reforms in Eastern Europe

Lange has written: 'One may well imagine a system in which production and the allocation of resources are guided by a

---

[1] Dobb, *On Economic Theory and Socialism*, London 1955, pp. 53–4.
[2] Sweezy, *Socialism*, New York 1949, p. 233.
[3] H. B. Chenery, 'Comparative Advantage and Economic Development', *The American Economic Review*, Vol. LI, no. 1, March 1961.

preference scale fixed by the Central Planning Board while the price system is used to distribute the consumers' goods produced. In such a system there is freedom of choice in consumption, but the consumers have no influence whatever on the decisions of the managers of production and of the productive resources.'[1] And he added: 'However, it does not seem very probable that such a system would be tolerated by the citizens of a socialist community.'[2] Strangely enough, the system he briefly outlined has been, in its main lines, the one adopted and used in all the centrally planned economies for a long time. Lange's original blueprint of a competitive socialist economy has had very little impact on the economic structure of those countries for which it was probably meant and which have, instead, resorted to a much more 'centralist' solution.

Until a few years ago, even the thought that eventually some compromise between the two models might be possible would have been quickly dismissed. The two systems seemed mutually incompatible. For Lange and Lerner consumers' preferences dictate the output of consumer goods and, therefore, influence the allocation of capital goods. In the Soviet-type model a central bureaucracy allocates most inputs and fixes the quantity of consumer goods available to the population. For Lange–Lerner, prices, be they market or accounting ones, are left to be determined by demand and supply. For Soviet planners, they arc fixed al the centre for all commodities and allowed to vary only by the use of taxation. The micro-economic preoccupations of Lange and Lerner, leading to a static, efficient and optimal allocation of resources, are in almost total contrast to the macro-economic aims of Soviet-type planners who are attempting to maximize the overall rate of growth of the economy, with little heed paid to calculations at the margin. Primacy of production replaces consumers' sovereignty, administrative direction the profit-maximizing activities of managers, total centralization the decentralized play of the market. And in the field of foreign trade quantitative, as opposed to price, considerations determine the structure of imports and exports, with only scanty attention given to comparative advantage and factor endowments. Cost differentials are replaced as criteria

[1] Lange and Taylor, 'Economic Theory of Socialism', p. 96.
[2] Ibid.

for foreign trade by the existence of shortages or surpluses in the economy.

But, as Lange himself later argued, there is no reason for this pattern to be the eternal institutional economic set-up of socialism. It is merely a historical necessity dictated by the conditions in which planning was started in the Soviet Union and in the Eastern European countries.[1] With the development of a more advanced and diversified economy, the aims of previous target planning and unbalanced growth in a few priority sectors have been, more or less, achieved; the continuance of high growth rates requires new organizations and institutions. In fact it is being gradually admitted that the present bureaucratic, over-centralized planning system is inhibiting growth prospects. In the Soviet Union Kantorovich estimated that the potential loss to the economy due to the system is somewhat between one-quarter to one-third of total output,[2] while in Czechoslovakia outdated planning methods probably contributed to the 1963 fall in national income.[3] Increasing attention is, therefore, being now paid to proposals for reform, and most of these focus on decentralization.

This does not mean that the Lange–Lerner system will automatically be soon adopted in the centrally planned economies. One basic difference, which no reform is likely to gloss over, is the central position of the plan in all communist countries, compared with its rather subordinate role in the competitive model. Even in Yugoslavia, where 'Professor Lange's model of market socialism, which was formulated by him in 1936–7 was the closest, in our opinion, to the Yugoslav model of economic system',[4] a plan, not merely coordinating the activities of various sectors, as the Lange–Lerner one would seem to do, but actually determining the development lines of the economy, is central to the economic structure.[5] A national

---

[1] Lange, 'Role of Planning in Socialist Economy', in Lange (ed.), *Problems of Political Economy of Socialism*, New Delhi 1962, pp. 17–19.

[2] A. Zauberman, 'New Winds in Soviet Planning', *Soviet Studies*, Vol. XII, No. 1, July 1960, p. 4.

[3] United Nations, Economic Commission for Europe, *Economic Survey of Europe in 1964*, Geneva 1965, Ch. 1, p. 2.

[4] I. M. Maksimovic, 'Professor Oskar Lange on Economic Theory of Socialism and Yugoslav Economic Thinking', *On Political Economy and Econometrics—Essays in honour of Oskar Lange*, Warsaw 1964, p. 349.

[5] A. Waterston, *Planning in Yugoslavia*, I.B.R.D., Baltimore 1962.

plan, therefore, deciding on the share of accumulation and consumption in national income, and on the distribution of investment among different *branches*,[1] will remain of paramount importance. Reforms will probably concentrate on giving much greater scope to the preferences of consumers, as opposed to those of planners, and allow a much more active play of market forces within the framework of the plan. This by itself will probably be sufficient to lead to far-reaching changes, such that the new systems will increasingly approximate many of the features of the Lange–Lerner one. It is likely that at the core of reforms will lie the changed role of the price mechanism, which can be regarded as an outstanding example of a decentralized organizational structure.[2] As long as the price system is not tampered with, no new incentive schemes (such as the one proposed recently in the Soviet Union by Liberman),[3] and no degree of purely functional decentralization (such as those implemented in Poland in 1956, in the Soviet Union in 1957 and in Czechoslovakia in 1959, and all more or less quickly repealed), will really solve the problem of excessive centralization and inflexibility. And once the first elements of a price reform are introduced it is unlikely that the process will stop halfway. Just as, in the words of Tinbergen, 'once you start to deviate from market price-formation you have to regulate more and more until the whole economy is regulated',[4] so too, once attempts are made to introduce some rationality into prices, planners may well be forced to go the whole way, or else piecemeal reforms will be of very limited use.

The first frank attempt to face the problem has come from Czechoslovakia, significantly the most developed of the Eastern European countries, and, therefore, the one most likely to be hampered by bureaucratic planning methods. The reforms, which began to be introduced in 1966, in many ways approximate features of both the Yugoslav and the Lange–Lerner

---

[1] Lange, 'Role of Planning in Socialist Economy', p. 22.

[2] L. Hurwicz, 'Conditions for Economic Efficiency of Centralized and Decentralized Economic Structures', in G. Grossman (ed.), *Value and Plan*, Berkeley and Los Angeles 1960, p. 164.

[3] United Nations, Economic Commission for Europe, *Economic Survey of Europe in 1962*, Geneva 1963, Part I, Ch. 1, pp. 45–8; and *Economic Survey of Europe in 1964*, Ch. 1, pp. 52–6.

[4] J. Tinbergen, 'Do Communist and Free Economies show a Converging Pattern?', *Soviet Studies*, Vol. XII, No. 4, August 1961, p. 340.

models.[1] Enterprise managers decide on inputs, outputs, product mix and on some investment within their concerns, by
following profit criteria and responding to market stimuli. The
plan lays down only the more general targets, though it still
allocates some of the investment fund. Prices of most commodities are left free to fluctuate according to demand and
supply, with ceilings introduced only in some cases and very
few prices actually fixed at the centre. In general, all micro-
economic decisions are left to the initiative of consumers and
managers while most macro-economic ones are still in central
hands. A similar pattern of reforms is taking place in foreign
trade. According to Lange–Lerner, international trade should
be dictated by comparative cost criteria, irrespective of whether
it is undertaken by a foreign trade monopoly or individual
enterprises. As long as prices were not used for allocation purposes and did not reflect opportunity costs, the scope for such an
approach in the centrally planned economies was limited and
other criteria had to be used. However, as soon as prices come
into their own again as indicators of scarcities, the criteria for
foreign trade become much clearer and simpler.

The Czech reforms would seem to be going in this direction,
by both freeing most prices from their previous controls and
letting them be determined by market forces, and by envisaging
a much higher degree of competition between domestic and
foreign producers through measures of import liberalization.
While in Lange–Lerner competition, both in the domestic
market and as against foreign suppliers, is an inherent part of
the model, in the centrally planned economies domestic competition has so far been severely limited, and foreign competition
has been non-existent. The much larger scope given to both
forms of competition in the Czech reforms will, in all likelihood,
result in market forces exerting a much greater influence on
both domestic and foreign trade production patterns and, therefore, lead to a closer approach to the ideals of the Lange–Lerner
model. This is not to say that several of the defects, outlined
above, of the Lange–Lerner approach to foreign trade will
be introduced lock, stock and barrel into Eastern European

---

[1] United Nations, Economic Commission for Europe, *Economic Survey of Europe in
1964*, Ch. 1, pp. 49–53; O. Sik, 'La gestion économique en Tchécoslovaquie',
Les Temps Modernes, 20e année, No. 229, June 1965; see also Chapter 3.

planning. It is highly likely that some degree of control over foreign trade will always be maintained, that the static comparative advantage pattern of today will not be blindly followed, and that, by the drawing up of perspective plans, a good deal of light will be shed on expected changes in the foreign trade structure of these countries.

The Lange–Lerner model, as a practical scheme rather than a theoretical one, is almost unattainable. On the other hand the over-centralized economic structure of the Soviet Union and of the Eastern European countries has outlived its function. Future needs and present reforms all point to some kind of compromise between the two which will maintain the planned direction of development, indispensable in economies where, after all, the means of production are in collective hands, while at the same time devoluting most of the functions of management to a decentralized structure. Nove says: 'There is always bound to be trouble along the lines at which the centralised portion of the plan meets the decentralised plans concocted by the enterprises',[1] but this trouble is likely to lead to much less waste than the inefficiency of the present system, and to be much more easily dealt with than the difficulties of setting up a perfect competition model of the Lange–Lerner kind.

[1] A. Nove, 'The Liberman Proposals', *Survey*, No. 47, April 1963, p. 117.

3

THE INSTITUTIONAL BACKGROUND

Before starting on an examination of the principles which have guided foreign trade in countries where central planning and public ownership of the means of production have become the main economic instruments of control (as opposed to the more theoretical cases previously considered), it is necessary to outline, if only very briefly, the institutional background on which foreign trade decisions have been taken. This background has, on the whole, been surprisingly similar for all these countries, despite the very different roles that foreign trade has played, and still plays, in, say, the Soviet Union or Hungary.[1] The early Soviet model, which was adopted just after the revolution and has been changed very little over the years since the first Five Year Plans,[2] was, more or less *in toto*, applied to the People's Democracies of Eastern Europe after 1945. A brief examination of Soviet foreign trade procedure and organization is, therefore, probably sufficient to illustrate the general practice of all the centrally planned economies, at least until the early 1960s. It is only recently that reform programmes have been discussed, notably in Czechoslovakia and Hungary, and 1966–7 saw the beginning of their implementation. These reforms, which will lead to quite radical changes in the organization of foreign trade, and are part of the much more general overhaul of, for instance, the whole Czech planning system, are likely to be followed in future by most of the other Eastern European countries, and their outline may well indicate the lines on which future changes in foreign trade structures may develop in, say, the DDR or Poland. Just as the Soviet model provided the blueprint to which Eastern European countries had to adapt themselves from 1945 onwards, so the Czech reforms may indicate the guiding lines along which changes may move in the future.

[1] N. Spulber, 'The Soviet Bloc Foreign Trade System', in M. Bornstein and D. R. Fusfeld (eds.), *The Soviet Economy—A Book of Readings*, Homewood, Ill. 1962, p. 295.
[2] N. Scott, Review of P. A. Chervyakov: *Organisatsiya i technika vneshnyei torgovli S.S.S.R.*, *Soviet Studies*, Vol. x, No. 4, April 1959, p. 394.

Soviet foreign trade institutions

At the basis of the Soviet model lies the principle of the foreign trade monopoly. Among the first actions of the Soviet revolutionary government were to take control of foreign trade (December 1917) and to nationalize it early in 1918.[1] Lenin justified this measure on the following three grounds: foreign trade was meant to defend the socialist economy against the offensive launched by the capitalist countries, was to be used to keep the production of the various sectors in balance and had to increase the defence potential of the USSR.[2] The principle of a foreign trade monopoly was, from then onwards, never abandoned, not even in the NEP days, and was further strengthened during the early period of the Five Year Plans. At present, responsibility for foreign trade is vested in a foreign trade ministry which co-ordinates all transactions with the rest of the world. Its main task is the construction of an import and export plan, compiled in strict co-operation with the central planning commission. In drawing up the import plan, the foreign trade ministry takes into account, on the one hand, the demands for imports made by enterprises to their industrial ministries and, on the other, the state of foreign markets and the supply estimates derived from the material balances communicated to it by Gosplan.[3] Bilateral treaties concluded with other socialist countries are integrated into this temporary plan which is then revised at both a higher (Gosplan) and at a lower (foreign trade corporations) level. The foreign trade ministry is thus the link between the supreme planning authority and the corporation which is actually engaged in foreign trade, just as industrial ministries, or *sovnarkhozy*, fulfil the same intermediate function in domestic planning. It sets general trade policy, in the form of both yearly and longer-term plans, and is responsible for the implementation of the current year's plan.[4]

Subordinated to the foreign trade ministry are the foreign

[1] P. A. Chervyakov, *Organisatsiya i technika vneshnyei torgovli S.S.S.R.*, Moscow 1962, pp. 24–5.
[2] T. Hermes, *Der Aussenhandel in den Ostblockstaaten*, Hamburg 1958, p. 17.
[3] E. Klinkmüller, *Die gegenwärtige Aussenhandelsverflechtung der Sowjetischen Besatzungszone Deutschlands*, Berlin 1959, pp. 13–14; A. Nove and D. Donnelly, *Trade with Communist Countries*, London 1960, pp. 21–2; F. L. Pryor, *The Communist Foreign Trade System*, London 1963, pp. 55–7; see also Chapter 4.
[4] Pryor, *Communist Foreign Trade System*, p. 245.

trade corporations. These corporations do the actual trading with foreign countries. Their number has usually fluctuated around twenty in all the Eastern European countries.[1] They are normally organized around various production sectors, so that each is responsible for the carrying out of imports and/or exports of given types of commodities, although some of them are responsible for specific trade problems, or geographical areas.[2] Their relationship to the foreign trade ministry is totally subordinate: volume, prices, transport costs, structure and direction of foreign trade have already been planned as far as possible by the ministry within the framework of the global trade plan. All these directives are merely forwarded to the foreign trade corporations who can, at best, suggest minor modifications.[3] Their links with the domestic enterprises which provide the exports, or purchase the imports, are very tenuous, so that the channels of contact are essentially vertical (from foreign trade ministry to foreign trade corporation, from industrial ministry to producing enterprise), and almost no horizontal contacts are allowed for, except at the very top level.

Each foreign trade corporation, given its commodity and/or country plan, will try to sell the quantities at its disposal or buy the required imports, or do both, at the best possible price on the foreign market. This is done through negotiations with foreign governments or firms. With capitalist countries the prices agreed upon are, usually, current world prices, though sometimes the Soviet Union sells below them. This is not so much due to deliberate dumping (on the contrary, Soviet trade delegates are considered very tough negotiators), but to the often erratic nature of Soviet exports—some unplanned surpluses come on to the market and if they are to be sold *en bloc* price cuts must be made.[4] Trade with the other Eastern European countries is also conducted on the basis of world prices—usually the world prices valid for some previous base year (for a long time the 1957–8, prices were in use,[5] but pressure to change them has mounted and 1960–4 world prices seem to have been

[1] Spulber, 'Soviet Bloc Foreign Trade System', p. 297.
[2] Pryor, *Communist Foreign Trade System*, p. 249.
[3] Spulber, 'Soviet Bloc Foreign Trade System', pp. 295–6.
[4] Nove and Donnelly, *Trade with Communist Countries*, pp. 24–5.
[5] F. D. Holzman, 'More on Soviet Bloc Trade Discrimination', *Soviet Studies*, Vol. XVII, No. 1, July 1965, pp. 61–2.

adopted since 1966).[1] It is said that these prices are corrected to take account of speculation, 'military inflationary pressure', etc. In other words, they are adjusted so as to avoid undue fluctuations. When world prices are indeterminate, or difficult to define, which is probably the case for most manufactured goods where quality differences are important, then bargaining and relative economic power are important in price fixing. At this point one could raise the question of price discrimination which, according to common belief, the Soviet Union has imposed on its smaller partners. This was certainly true for the period up to about 1954. Since then, some of the data available could suggest a continuation of this practice,[2] but such a conclusion is based only on comparisons of prices charged in intra-socialist trade and world prices. The fact that prices in intra-socialist trade may be adjusted to the specific comparative advantage situation existing in the bloc (as Eastern European economists say they are), is not considered. It has been shown that if such specific comparative advantage situations differ from those in the rest of the world, and if they are taken into account in price setting, then the apparent price discrimination practised by the Soviet Union may not exist.[3]

In their internal operations the corporations buy the commodity they are expected to sell at its wholesale domestic price (in, say, roubles) and then sell it abroad at the world (or contract) price. The foreign currency they receive is deposited and

[1] *The Financial Times*, 17 Feb. 1966, p. 5; *The Economist*, 18 June 1966, p. 1295.

[2] H. Mendershausen, 'Terms of Trade between the Soviet Union and the smaller Communist Countries, 1955–7', *The Review of Economics and Statistics*, Vol. XLI, No. 2, May 1959; and 'The terms of Soviet-Satellite Trade: A Broadened Analysis', *The Review of Economics and Statistics*, Vol. XLII, No. 2, May 1960.

[3] F. D. Holzman, 'Soviet Foreign Trade Pricing and the question of Discrimination: A "Customs Union" Approach', *The Review of Economics and Statistics*, Vol. XLIV, No. 2, May 1962; and 'More on Soviet Bloc Trade Discrimination'. Lately, it could even be argued, price discrimination has gone the other way, if it is true that specialization in raw materials is becoming very costly to the Soviet Union. In any case, it has been argued by Soviet and Polish economists that the raw material prices used in CMEA trade should be above world prices, suggesting that the terms of trade, following world market developments, have turned against the primary producing countries of the area. Though only of secondary importance, this is likely to strengthen Rumania's position in its dispute with the other CMEA members. United Nations, Economic Commission for Europe, *Economic Bulletin for Europe*, Vol. XVIII, No. 1, November 1966, pp. 13–14; F. D. Holzman, 'Background and Origin of the Rumanian Dispute with Comecon', *Soviet Studies*, Vol. XVI, No. 2, October 1964.

converted, at the official rate of exchange, at the State Bank; vice versa for imports—the import is bought abroad with foreign currency sold to the foreign trade corporation by the State Bank at the official rate of exchange, and is then sold on the internal market at the wholesale price of similar goods produced at home.

Two problems arise. One is the setting of a home price for an import which is not produced domestically. If the price is set at a level which is relatively low, then the demand for the commodity is likely to increase rapidly and the import would be substituted for whatever domestic products were used in its place beforehand. The opposite would happen in the case of a price that had been set too high. Though such changes in demand will not lead directly to immediate changes in imports, ultimately import plans are based on the stated needs of enterprises. The second problem arises when the foreign trade corporation makes a loss or a profit on its transactions. This is highly likely, given the artificial nature of the rate of exchange. There is no guarantee that the proceeds of a sale abroad, converted at the official rate, will cover the purchase price of the good at home, and if they do not the exporting corporation will have made a loss. On the other hand, it is possible for a commodity bought abroad to sell for a much higher price at home, so that the importing corporation makes a profit. This is the most likely pattern in practice, as the official rate of exchange has been, as a rule, overvalued. Unless, therefore, the elasticity of demand for goods exported by Eastern European countries is very low, the state will have to subsidize the exporting organizations, while the profit of the importing ones will be paid out to it. No real significance can, however, be attributed to this. It does not mean, for instance, that the centrally planned countries exercise large-scale organized dumping, as has often been thought, since both export subsidies and import levies are only due to the artificial nature of the rate of exchange and to the total divorce between the internal economy and the world market, a divorce begun, in the Soviet Union at least, as early as 1926–7.[1]

---

[1] F. D. Holzman, 'Some Financial Aspects of Soviet Foreign Trade', Joint Economic Committee, Congress of the United States, *Comparisons of the United States and Soviet Economies*, Washington 1959, Part II, pp. 429–32.

A further characteristic of Soviet-type foreign trade has been, and still is, its insistence on bilateralism. There are two main reasons for this, both linked to the quantitative nature of Soviet planning. Firstly, once trade contracts with a specific partner have been signed, one knows what goods one will acquire and what goods one must produce for export. If trade were to be multilateral, i.e. if a balance due from country A to country B in respect of a surplus of imports over exports could be transferred by B to the account of country C, the latter could demand in settlement goods whose export or excess production had not been planned for in A. If stocks were abundant or the productive machine flexible, such an unplanned demand could probably be met, but in the conditions of rigid planning prevalent in Eastern Europe any unexpected demand is likely to throw production plans out of gear. Secondly, having bilateral contracts, at least with other planned economies, makes it easier to ensure fulfilment of one's own import plan. Take, for example, the case of country A being slow in fulfilling its export deliveries to country B. B, in its turn, could then threaten A with withholding supplies, thereby exerting some pressure on A's economy to be more prompt. On the other hand, the rigid character of trade fixed bilaterally means that each time something unexpected happens, import and export plans have to be revised, normally in a hurry. This has predictable consequences on an already strained planning machine. In these conditions foreign trade, instead of contributing to the plan's elasticity, achieves the opposite result.[1]

Payment arrangements between centrally planned economies have, so far, normally assumed annual bilateral balancing of current payments, but a multilateral payment scheme for CMEA, rather similar to the old European Payments Union, came into operation in 1964,[2] 'the aim of which is to ensure that in the future each member country will be obliged to aim at balancing of current payments (subject to any long-term credit available) only with the CMEA area as a whole, instead of—as heretofore—with each member individually. Transactions will

[1] J. M. Colette, 'Le blocage de la croissance économique tchécoslovaque', *Cahiers de l'I.S.E.A.*, Série G (No. 22), No. 168, December 1965, p. 134.
[2] United Nations, Economic Commission for Europe, *Economic Bulletin for Europe*, Vol. xvi, No. 2, November 1964, p. 44.

in future take place in "transferable roubles" through accounts with the "International Co-operation Bank" newly established in Moscow...'.[1] The operations of the CMEA bank have not, however, been very numerous and, notwithstanding quota payments by member countries in gold and foreign exchange, its main function would seem limited to that of balancing residuals of the bilateral deals which still overwhelmingly characterize intra-area trade.[2] As for payment arrangements with market economies, they vary quite widely, with trading in convertible currencies as the most used form, though some barter arrangements are still common.[3]

The most striking characteristic of the foreign trade organization of Eastern European countries, and that by which they differ most from market economies, is the almost total insulation of the domestic market from the world one. A general world depression, of the 1929 kind, would (and did) have an effect on a centrally planned economy, in so far as it would lead to some drastic changes in foreign trade volume and, therefore, in domestic output. But normal trade or price fluctuations, which in market economies are associated with financial and 'real' effects in each country, are completely absorbed in Eastern Europe by the organizational set-up. The effects of inflationary pressures at home on the balance of payments, or of changes in foreign demand on the domestic employment or output situation, are avoided by the system of export subsidies and import levies (isolating domestic and foreign price structures from each other), and by the quantitative nature of foreign trade planning. Thus, in the DDR it would seem that, at least at certain times, two balances of payments were calculated, one in roubles, based on world prices, the other in DM (East) based on home prices.[4]

Movements in exchange rates do not affect foreign trade to any marked degree either (they may, at best, increase or decrease foreign exchange revenues from tourism). Though devaluations would probably bring foreign and home prices closer, this would not entail the changes in foreign trade flows

[1] Ibid. p. 45.
[2] *The Economist*, 18 June 1966, p. 1295.
[3] United Nations, Economic Commission for Europe, *Economic Bulletin for Europe*, Vol. XVI, No. 2, p. 45.
[4] Klinkmüller, *Die gegenwärtige Aussenhandelsverflechtung*, p. 42.

usually associated with devaluations in market economies.[1] The only field in which foreign trade can have some influence on the internal situation is the financial one, since the balance of subsidies versus levies in the 'domestic' balance of payments can affect the total supply of money, if actual trade differs from trade plans.[2] Tariffs, and the other mechanisms by which market economies protect themselves from foreign competition, play no part in the foreign trade organization of Eastern European countries. Some kinds of tariffs do, however, exist in the Soviet Union, the DDR, Czechoslovakia, Poland and Hungary, and are used with purely discriminatory aims, in order to encourage foreign trade corporations, given their commodity plans, to buy from (or sell to) those countries not subject to duty. In Hungary and the Soviet Union they were apparently introduced to counteract the discriminatory effects of the Common Market and may well be used as a lever in future trade negotiations.[3]

Present reform trends in Eastern Europe

The system so far outlined has been increasingly subject to heavy criticism. The high degree of centralization implicit in a foreign trade plan elaborated at the national level had several advantages in the past, when target planning necessitated a foreign trade structure little concerned with relative costs and prices (which were distorted in any case), and when radical changes in the structure of trade and production had to be made in a relatively short time. But centralization also had disadvantages, which increased as the economy became more complex. The system, for instance, lacked the flexibility to meet new day-to-day opportunities and seldom encouraged an expansion in the volume of foreign trade.[4] The lack of contact between the foreign trade corporations and enterprises made it difficult to channel the knowledge of new markets or oppor-

---

[1] M. Bornstein, 'The Reform and Revaluation of the Ruble', *The American Economic Review*, Vol. LI, No. 1, March 1961, pp. 117–22.

[2] E. Ames, 'The Exchange Rate in Soviet-type Economies', *The Review of Economics and Statistics*, Vol. XXXV, No. 4, November 1953; Pryor, *Communist Foreign Trade System*, pp. 267–70.

[3] United Nations, Economic Commission for Europe, *Economic Bulletin for Europe*, Vol. XVI, No. 2, pp. 43–4.

[4] Pryor, *Communist Foreign Trade System*, p. 75.

tunities, which a corporation might have, to an enterprise which should have increased its production.[1] Nor were enterprises terribly interested in exportable commodities, since incentives were geared mainly to the quantitative fulfilment and over-fulfilment of a domestic plan and not to successful sales abroad, which would have necessitated a much greater concern with quality.

Proposals for reform thus began to be made as early as 1953, when in the DDR, for instance, some large enterprises were permitted to export directly to non-communist countries.[2] Similar reforms were made in Hungary in 1956–7.[3] At the same time, horizontal communications between foreign trade corporations and producers were strengthened in East Germany.[4] Most of these changes were revoked later in the 1950s, but in 1960 special premiums and bonus schemes for exports were introduced in East German and Hungarian enterprises.[5] A similar type of reform was introduced in Poland in 1962,[6] while even in the Soviet Union it was argued that domestic price structures should be more responsive to foreign ones,[7] and some foreign trade decentralization was encouraged.[8]

But real decentralization of decisions and removal of the strict separation between trade and production enterprises have so far been proposed only in Czechoslovakia (and, to a lesser extent, in Hungary) as part of the general economic reforms which came into operation from 1966 onwards. The aim of these reforms is to increase the volume, and even more the efficiency, of foreign trade, to provide foreign trade operations with a much larger degree of flexibility, to stimulate the search for less quantitatively orientated criteria for trading and slowly to close the gap between foreign and domestic price

---

[1] I. Agoston, *Le Marché Commun Communiste*, Paris 1965, pp. 124–6.
[2] Pryor, *Communist Foreign Trade System*, pp. 82–3.
[3] L. Zsoldos, *The Economic Integration of Hungary in the Soviet Bloc: Foreign Trade Experience*, Columbus, Ohio 1963, p. 13.
[4] Pryor, *Communist Foreign Trade System*, pp. 82–3.
[5] United Nations, Economic Commission for Europe, *Economic Survey of Europe in 1960*, Geneva 1961, p. 17.
[6] United Nations, Economic Commission for Europe, *Economic Survey of Europe in 1962*, Geneva 1963, Part I, Ch. I, p. 49.
[7] Ibid. p. 48.
[8] G. Adler-Karlsson, 'Some notes on the Foreign Trade Decisions in the U.S.S.R.', *Øst Økonomi*, No. 3–4, 1961, pp. 2–5.

structures, so as to decrease the degree of isolation of the Czech economy.[1] To this end, the importance of the foreign trade ministry will be reduced. It will still draw up long-run plans together with the industrial ministries and the central planning commission, but the yearly plans that it will forward to the foreign trade corporations will have lost their detailed character. They will be broad plans calculated in value terms, with detailed instructions limited only to those bilateral contracts already entered into and to some import specifications for a few sectors. Apart from this the corporations will be able to operate freely, selecting the best structure and direction of both imports and exports. Exports will be purchased directly from the producers and, to encourage their output, the corporations will themselves provide incentives (some of them even in foreign currency), should the sale of some given commodity prove to be advantageous. Import needs will also be negotiated between enterprises and foreign trade corporations, subject to some balance of payments constraint, and here too, bonuses will go to those plants that achieve a certain degree of import substitution.

Since no alterations are envisaged in the rate of exchange, the old problem of subsidies for exports and levies on imports will remain but, to encourage foreign trade efficiency, the character of subsidies and levies will be changed. If, for instance, a foreign trade corporation had, up to now, purchased a commodity at an internal price of 100 kĉs, and had sold it abroad at the equivalent of 40 kĉs, it would receive from now onwards a maximum subsidy of 60 kĉs. If it were in the course of the following year to receive a lower price abroad, it would have to sustain the loss from its own funds. However, if it were to obtain a better price, it would be able to retain for itself part of the full subsidy which it would still get from the budget, though it would have to forward part of this to the producing enterprise, since the better economic result would probably be due to higher quality. In the following planning period, however, the subsidy would now be based on the difference between the domestic price and the new, higher price received abroad. Thus, the amount of the

---

[1] F. Hamouz, 'Foreign Trade under the New System of Planned Management', translated from Czech (*Nova Mysl*, No. 11, 1964), in *American Review of Soviet and Eastern European Foreign Trade*, Vol. 1, No. 6, November–December 1965.

subsidy will be based on a (sliding) yearly average and should gradually decrease as efficiency improves. For imports the same process will work in reverse. The aim is eventually to close the gap between foreign and domestic prices. A second way in which this aim will be furthered will be by allowing a larger quantity of imports on the domestic market (especially in the so-far-neglected consumer goods sector), so as to stimulate a higher degree of efficiency and a faster rate of technical progress in the backward domestic sectors.[1] It is envisaged that in some branches foreign competition could even wipe out domestic industry, but this is regarded as inevitable. The difficulties with this kind of approach lie in the shortage of foreign currency at the disposal of the Czech economy, and in the possibility that such a policy could produce unemployment, even if only of a temporary nature.

Another model of foreign trade organization for a centrally planned economy is provided by Yugoslavia. It is at the opposite end of the spectrum from the early Soviet-type model, and has lately become almost indistinguishable from a market economy. For a time Yugoslavia, though avoiding the total insulation of the other Eastern European countries, maintained an elaborate system of multiple rates of exchange and foreign trade monopolies, so as to protect the domestic price structure. But in 1960 a uniform exchange rate (and a set of customs duties) were introduced, and this, together with the practice of letting most enterprises deal directly with foreign customers or sellers, makes the Yugoslav model very different from even the new Czech one, and rules out, for the moment at least, any likelihood of a wholesale application of the Yugoslav system in the centrally planned economies.[2]

Most of the CMEA countries are, however, envisaging some alterations in their planning structure, or are already introducing them.[3] A common characteristic of practically all the changes is the attempt to close the gap existing at present

[1] O. Sik, 'Problems of the New System of Planned Management', *Czechoslovak Economic Papers*, No. 5, Prague 1965, pp. 30–2.

[2] United Nations, Economic Commission for Europe, *Economic Survey of Europe in 1960*, p. 56; and *Economic Bulletin for Europe*, Vol. xvi, No. 2, pp. 46–7.

[3] Since Rumania has lately caught up with the general industrial reform movement (*Le Monde*, 18 October 1967, p. 3), the only Eastern European country left with the old planning techniques is now Albania.

between producers and foreign trade enterprises. This aim is being pursued either by letting selected firms deal directly with foreign customers or else by allowing some measure of decentralization in foreign trade planning. Prospects for reform seem, therefore, to lie in the direction at present being followed by Czechoslovakia. A few years ago the chosen model would still have been that of the largest socialist state—the Soviet Union. Nowadays, though Russia's planning mechanism is changing, it is changing all too slowly, and it is much more likely that the more drastic and enterprising changes attempted in the most developed and industrialized of the Eastern European countries—Czechoslovakia—will serve, if not as a blueprint, at least as an indicator of future trends.

4

THE SOVIET EXPERIENCE—
MATERIAL BALANCES AND THE
DRIVE TO AUTARKY

The amount of material on foreign trade published in the Soviet Union and the Eastern European countries before 1956 is very limited. Apart from a few statistics and some descriptions of the organization of the foreign trade ministry, there is an almost total lack of discussion of the more important problems of planning foreign trade and deciding on the structure of imports and exports. This is partly due to the autarkic tendencies of the time, i.e. to the minor role which international trade was held to play, and partly to the lack of any well-formulated theory supporting the existing pattern of exchanges.

The Soviet model of foreign trade planning

It seems, from what evidence one can collect, that for both Eastern Europe and the Soviet Union the foreign trade plan was an appendage of the national plan, linked to the latter by the method of material balances. This method, which lay at the basis of planning in communist economies from the early days of Lenin's electrification plan,[1] is supposed, according to Soviet economists, to have inspired the young Leontief, while still in Russia, to the eventual development of his input–output tables.[2] Be that as it may, the fact remains that the material balances system has developed very little from its early days and is now far behind the more sophisticated input–output techniques of the West.

It consists, essentially, of a centrally operated macro-

---

[1] M. R. Eidel'man, *Statistika materialno-technichesko snabzheniya*, Moscow 1953, p. 188.

[2] According to Nemchinov, Leontief was especially influenced by the 'Balance of the National Economy of the U.S.S.R. for 1923–4'; V. S. Nemchinov, editorial preface to: L. V. Kantorovich, *The Best Use of Economic Resources*, Oxford 1965, p. ix.

economic balancing of demand and supply, for all or most industrial products, in physical rather than value terms. For any given commodity, the central planning agency draws up a budget of estimated production, stocks at the beginning of the planning period and imports, and compares it to estimated consumption, ascertained by applying technical coefficients (similar to the technological input–output ratios) to the industries using the commodity in question, and adding exports and stocks at the end of the period. The aim is to make total availabilities coincide with total needs. In the first stage, the planned output of, say, sector I is distributed to the other industries using the particular good. These, given their inputs, proceed to frame their output plans, which will in turn be distributed to other consuming industries. The problem of consistency almost inevitably arises at this point, since the outputs of sectors II, III, etc., may not be sufficient to satisfy the input needs of sector I. By successive iterations, however, a consistent plan should eventually emerge.[1] But the number of iterations needed to achieve a high degree of consistency may be too large (it must be remembered that the availability of computers still seems to be rather limited in the Soviet Union). Iteration is, therefore, often stopped short and other methods of a more direct kind are employed to make demand tally with supply. Pressures may, for instance, be put on some of the coefficients to force industries to economize on the input side (in official phraseology this is called 'mobilization of internal resources'), allocations to non-priority sectors may be cut down, substitution between materials, if feasible, may be encouraged or, finally, planned imports may be stepped up (or exports cut).[2]

---

[1] H. Hirsch, *Mengenplanung und Preisplanung in der Sowjetunion*, Tübingen 1957; J. M. Montias, 'Planning with Material Balances in Soviet-type Economies', *The American Economic Review*, Vol. XLIX, No. 5, December 1959; H. S. Levine, 'The Centralized Planning of Supply in Soviet Industry' in M. Bornstein and D. R. Fusfeld (eds.), *The Soviet Economy—A Book of Readings*, Homewood, Ill. 1962; 'Input-Output Analysis and Soviet Planning', *The American Economic Review*, Vol. LII, No. 2 (Papers and Proceedings), May 1962; P. J. D. Wiles, *The Political Economy of Communism*, Oxford 1962, Ch. 10; A. Bergson, *The Economics of Soviet Planning*, New Haven 1964, Ch. 7; United Nations, Economic Commission for Europe, 'Economic Planning in Europe', *Economic Survey of Europe in 1962*, Geneva 1965, Part II, Ch. 4, pp. 23–31.

[2] Levine, 'The Centralized Planning', pp. 98–100.

The system does not start with final demand. For a long time this would have been considered as a major methodological sin. Nowadays proponents of final-demand planning exist, but can be accused of a 'consumption oriented approach' which would conflict with the traditional emphasis on growth.[1] Usually, therefore, planning begins with the setting of targets for some 'leading links', or priority sectors, functioning as the determinants of other outputs, which then follow by technical necessity.[2] Given, therefore, the planners' preferences, reflected in the choice of the priority sectors, and given the theoretical possibility of a consistent plan,[3] the material balances technique can, just like an input–output table, arrive at quantities of goods that are consistent with each other, but it cannot provide criteria for deciding whether one production mix is better than another.

In practice, however, a fully consistent plan is never drawn up, since the simultaneous inversion of the material balances matrix is not feasible. (The whole table is expressed in physical and not in value terms and does not necessarily form an interlocking set; there is not always an equal number of rows and columns, and sometimes rows represent products and columns ministries.) And iteration, as explained above, is so cumbersome a process that it is never pursued beyond the third or, at best, fourth stage, with little importance being attached to indirect requirements.[4] Further, as the technical difficulties of setting up and iterating material balances grew, the range of items covered was cut down and comprehensiveness was thereby reduced.[5] Other defects of the system arise from failures in the transmission to higher authorities of information about production functions, and failures in the production plan itself.[6] In fact, the moment output plans are not fulfilled in one branch (quite a common event in Soviet planning), and the distribution

---

[1] V. G. Treml, 'Input-Output Analysis and Soviet Planning', in J. P. Hardt et al. (eds.), *Mathematics and Computers in Soviet Economic Planning*, New Haven 1967, p. 104.

[2] Wiles, *Political Economy of Communism*, p. 197.

[3] Montias, 'Planning with Material Balances', pp. 967–74.

[4] Wiles, *Political Economy of Communism*, p. 197; B. A. Balassa, *The Hungarian Experience in Economic Planning*, New Haven 1959, p. 66.

[5] A. Zauberman, *Industrial Progress in Poland, Czechoslovakia and East Germany—1937–1962*, London 1964, p. 5.

[6] Montias, 'Planning with Material Balances', pp. 977–?

of this output does not proceed along the lines laid down by the balances, the whole system, because of its inherent inflexibility and reliance on 'tight' planning, breaks down.

Despite all these shortcomings, planning by balances is still at the core of planning in Soviet-type economies and determines to a significant extent the foreign trade plan of these countries. The mechanism by which the latter is dependent on the former is exceedingly simple—if the material balances show a deficit for some commodity, recourse will be made to imports; if they show a surplus, this will be exported. Since surpluses, in the conditions of tight planning common to all the communist countries, were unlikely,[1] what happened was that, once the import needs had been determined by the material balances, then exports would be planned so as to pay for them, thus introducing the necessity for a new iteration process in order to reach consistency.[2] As two Hungarian economists put it: 'an import plan is worked out on the basis of the production plan and an export plan on the basis of the import and production plans'.[3] Spulber describes it more vividly: 'the dynamics of the plan determine the dynamics of imports, which in their turn condition the dynamics of exports'.[4]

Such a simplified planning procedure can be linked to the post-revolutionary desire for a lower degree of dependence on the West, which was transformed by Stalin in the middle 1930s, into a conscious autarkic policy for the Soviet Union,

---

[1] Unless actually planned for, as in the case of some staple commodities (see below, pp. 54–6).

[2] Almost exactly the opposite policy seems to have been followed in China where, at least during the 1950s, imports were planned as a function of export capacity. In this respect China behaved more like the average less-developed country, dependent on its foreign currency earnings to fulfil its import plan, than like a Soviet-type economy. The Soviet Union was able, partly, to avoid such a policy, because of its greater self-sufficiency (and willingness to sell agricultural products even in times of famine at home), while the smaller Eastern European countries were helped by the existence of a world socialist market with a ready demand for many of their exports. For the Chinese example see D. H. Perkins, 'The International Impact on Chinese Central Planning' and A. Eckstein, 'Foreign Trade of China: A Summary Appraisal', both in A. A. Brown and E. Neuberger (eds.), *International Trade and Central Planning*, Berkeley and Los Angeles 1968.

[3] T. Liska and A. Marias, 'Optimum Returns and International Division of Labour', translated excerpts from the Hungarian (*Közgazdasagi Szemle*, No. 1, 1954) in: United Nations, Economic Commission for Europe, *Economic Survey of Europe in 1954*, Geneva 1955, p. 133.

[4] Spulber, *The Economics of Communist Eastern Europe*, New York 1957, p. 153.

and was imposed on to the Eastern European countries after
World War II. One has recourse to imports only if these are
fundamentally necessary to the economy, once all possible
domestic sources of supply have been exhausted. One engages
in international trade only in so far as one cannot avoid it, i.e.
practically only in order to obtain non-competing imports.
Beyond that point, autarky is the only possible policy since
it avoids most forms of dependence on 'unreliable' foreign
suppliers. It is a characteristic of a planned economy of the
Soviet type that this desire for autarky is not just apparent on
an international scale but is paralleled in the autarky drives
of industrial ministries or *sovnarchozy*, which aim to produce as
many as possible of the inputs they need within their own
administration or region. It is, of course, true that planners
generally dislike uncertainty and that foreign trade can be a
major source of uncertainty, so that planning may be defined
as 'inward looking',[1] but other factors also existed to explain
the Soviet Union's retreat into autarky.[2]

This principle that 'the fundamental determinant is our need
for imports...we plan imports and then plan to export enough
to pay for them', referred to by Oskar Lange as the first basic
principle of socialist international trade,[3] can be put into a very
simplified mathematical form, of an input–output type, showing
the possibility of consistency.[4] In such a model, as suggested by
Levine,[5] exports would play the role of an intermediate product,
since their function is that of obtaining imports. But the application of such schemes to the Eastern European or Soviet economies is hindered by the practical difficulties which meet any
attempt to apply input–output techniques in communist
countries. For almost ten years such techniques have been
known and experimented with in the Soviet Union, for example,
but up to date they have not been integrated with the other

[1] B. Balassa, 'Planning in an Open Economy', *Kyklos*, Vol. xix, No. 3, 1966, p. 385.
[2] H. S. Levine, 'The Effects of Foreign Trade on Soviet Planning Practices' in Brown and Neuberger (eds.), *International Trade*, p. 258.
[3] Quoted in Wiles, 'Changing Economic Thought in Poland', *Oxford Economic Papers*, Vol. ix, No. 2, June 1957, p. 201.
[4] A. Boltho, *An Examination of Foreign Trade Criteria in Socialist Economies*, unpub-lished B.Litt. dissertation, Oxford University 1967, Ch. 4.
[5] Levine, 'The Effects of Foreign Trade on Soviet Planning Practices', *International Trade*, pp. 271–2.

more traditional tools of planning. As mentioned above, one key difficulty lies in the point of departure of the planning process—present methods consist in the extrapolation of the gross output levels of a few key sectors, with national income magnitudes left as a residual; input–output would require the reversal of this process and would probably, though not necessarily, shift the emphasis from the traditional sectors (basically Department 1 goods),[1] to more consumption-oriented ones. This would involve a study of how to plan demand—a branch of economics which has only recently been rediscovered in Eastern Europe.[2]

In any case, the system does not really work in quite the simple way so far described. There are many factors that distort or alter the 'imports first, exports planned to pay for them' approach, both in the Soviet Union and in Eastern Europe. For the Soviet Union, as Holzman puts it,

conceptually it is useful to divide Soviet imports into two classes: goods which are unavailable in required amounts in the USSR... and those which could be produced but not as quickly as desired or at low enough cost...Similarly, exports can be conceived as falling into two classes: permanent and temporary. The permanent exports (are)...commodities easy to produce in surplus for export, for which there are steady markets. These exports can be viewed as paying for part or all of permanent imports. In addition, the USSR has to export many other commodities to finance the remainder of their imports. This class of exports ranges from commodities in which the

[1] The division of production into two categories is a feature of Marx's economic analysis which has been adopted in Eastern European planning. Department 1 goods are all the goods which are used in the process of production while Department 11 covers goods for consumption. A similar distinction is used for industrial products only: Group A goods or producers' goods and Group B or consumer goods; A. Nove, *The Soviet Economy*, London 1961, pp. 260–3.

[2] There has been a revival of interest in the theory of consumption during the last few years whose reasons are likely to be both technical and economic. On the technical side, the growing interest in input–output analysis has probably stimulated the study of final demand structures; on the politico-economic side, the emphasis put by present reformers on consumers' choice is encouraging the study of such long-ignored concepts as income elasticities and is paving the way for future econometric research; Zauberman, 'On the Objective Function for the Soviet Economy', *Economica*, Vol. xxxii, No. 127, August 1965, p. 323; Treml, 'Input-Output Analysis', pp. 105–7; E. J. Mishan and A. Zauberman, 'Resurrection of the Concept of Consumers' Choice', in Zauberman, *Aspects of Planometrics*, London 1967, p. 39.

Soviet Union has a short run advantage vis-à-vis specific trading partners...to commodities which are not produced by plan in surplus but which are in temporary surplus or are diverted from internal needs to pay for essential imports.[1]

A similar view is put forward by Nove.[2] For imports, therefore, the simple picture sketched above remains partially true: planners do attempt to import only non-competing goods. For exports, however, the picture can be quite different. At times, it is true, the foreign trade ministry does not look for profitability or economic advantage but 'sometimes one uses for export a commodity less profitable but at the same time less needed by the Soviet Union or not in shortage (ne defitsitnii)'.[3] At other times, however, just the opposite course may be followed. In the early 1930s, for instance, despite widespread famine in the Ukraine, grain was exported to pay for the imports needed for the First Five Year Plan.[4] Similarly, in the early post-war years the Soviet Union exported food and raw materials to the Eastern European countries, even though its own needs for such commodities, just after the war, were probably as pressing as those of its newly found political allies.[5] And recently the Soviet Union seems to have been using some of its stockpiles of commodities, other than gold, as international reserves to solve balance of payments difficulties.[6]

A further instance which seems to work against the declared autarkic policies of the Soviet Union is the trade (and aid) conducted with less-developed countries. Here exports are primarily (in fact almost exclusively) composed of machinery and industrial equipment, while imports are mostly primary products and raw materials not always absolutely necessary to the Soviet Union (as, for instance, in the case of Burmese

[1] F. D. Holzman, 'Foreign Trade', in A. Bergson and S. Kuznets (eds.), *Economic Trends in the Soviet Union*, Cambridge, Mass. 1963, pp. 302–3 (footnote 21).

[2] A. Nove and D. Donnelly, *Trade with Communist Countries*, London 1960, pp. 21–2.

[3] Institut Mezhdunarodnich Otnoshenyi (Institute for International Relations), *Organisatsiya i technika vneshnyei torgovli S.S.S.R. i drugich sotsialisticheskich stran*, Moscow 1963, p. 162.

[4] H. Schwartz, *Russia's Soviet Economy*, London 1957, p. 508.

[5] M. Dewar, *Soviet Trade with Eastern Europe, 1945–1949*, London 1951, pp. 28–9.

[6] O. Hoeffding, 'Recent Structural Changes and Balance-of-Payments Adjustments in Soviet Foreign Trade', in Brown and Neuberger (eds.), *International Trade*.

rice, or Cuban sugar).[1] As an expert on the Soviet aid programme puts it: 'the approach seems to be: tell us what you
want and we will take anything you wish to sell to us in
exchange'.[2] In so far as long-term trade contracts are a com-
ponent of plans and in so far as they specify, at the moment of
negotiation, the exact nature of imports and exports, some
exports must clearly be planned in advance, in order to satisfy
a stipulated future demand, and investments must be directed
into such sectors. In fact, the process of getting rid of surpluses,
outlined above, is probably restricted to one-year plans.
Within the spectrum of short-run planning, unforeseen con-
tingencies may have to be met by unforeseen residuals; but for
five-year plans, the planning of both exports and imports
probably takes place concomitantly, the more so now that
national plans are being co-ordinated and long-run specialization and trade agreements signed under the auspices of CMEA.

In Eastern Europe the foreign trade planning process seems
to have been very similar to the Soviet one, at least in the earlier
post-war years, notwithstanding the very important differences
in economic structure between, on the one hand, almost self-
sufficient Russia and, on the other, the very foreign-trade-
dependent 'satellite' countries.[3] In Poland: 'exports of very
many goods are a resultant item of the material balances'.[4]
In Hungary, while imports were determined by the plan,
exports were haphazardly chosen: "The only criterion for the
volume and composition of exports has been whether or not
they pay for imports regardless of price.'[5] A similar situation
existed in the DDR where, again, imports and exports depended
on the state of the material balances.[6]

But here, too, other elements cloud the simple picture. Just

---

[1] J. S. Berliner, *Soviet Economic Aid*, New York 1958; H. Chambre, 'La doctrine
Soviétique concernant les pays du "Tiers Monde"', *Cahiers de l'I.S.E.A.*, Série G
(No. 13), No. 124, April 1962, pp. 12–16.

[2] Berliner, *Soviet Economic Aid*, p. 146.

[3] A Czech economist even went so far as to describe the adaptation of national
foreign trade planning policies to the Soviet pattern as 'an indiscriminate imitation of the historically conditioned example of the Soviet Union'; V. Kaigl,
'International Division of Labour in the World Socialist System', *Czechoslovak
Economic Papers*, No. 1, Prague 1959, p. 11.

[4] Montias, *Central Planning in Poland*, New Haven 1962, p. 99.

[5] L. Zsoldos, *The Economic Integration of Hungary into the Soviet Bloc: Foreign Trade
Experience*, Columbus, Ohio 1963, p. 11.

[6] F. L. Pryor, *Communist Foreign Trade System*, pp. 57–60.

to hope that surpluses would arise here and there, when the involvement in foreign trade was so much greater than Russia's would have been too risky a policy. Exports had to be planned more carefully and it appears that attention was given, when choosing the composition of exports, to foreign demand conditions, as well as to the possibilities for expanding domestic production and/or restraining consumption.[1] Since trade was much more important before the war in Eastern Europe than in Russia, exports often consisted of commodities that had been traditionally sold abroad and for which, therefore, it could be presumed that some comparative advantage still existed. (The major difference was that the direction of trade changed markedly, the Soviet Union becoming by far the most important buyer.) While in Russia, if a sector showed a surplus not needed at home, investment in that branch would probably be trimmed in the next planning period,[2] in Eastern European countries investment in industries producing surpluses for export was often fostered, despite the drive towards autarky.

Further, just as for the USSR, the continuing increase in the importance of trade contracts made perspective foreign trade planning more vital. From a 'virtual barter of residuals',[3] trade flows within CMEA have progressively taken on a more economic character and are based, at present, on specialization agreements and long-term contracts, as well as on more refined calculations of foreign trade efficiency. The material balances technique of foreign trade planning is rapidly losing ground, while even more inflexible theories, such as the following: 'in the determination of the direction and composition (of foreign trade) primary role is given to...political objectives which cannot be quantified. Therefore the views of those who want to develop the objectives of foreign trade solely on grounds of economic considerations are incorrect',[4] if ever adhered to, have definitely been superseded.

[1] T. P. Alton, *Polish post-war Economy*, New York 1955, p. 266.
[2] Nove and Donnelly, *Trade with Communist Countries*, p. 40.
[3] M. C. Kaser, *Comecon* (2nd edition), London 1967, p. 177.
[4] G. Karady, 'Calculation of the Economic Character of Foreign Trade', translated excerpts from the Hungarian (*Közgazdasagi Szemle*, No. 2, 1959) in Zsoldos, *Economic Integration of Hungary*, p. 90.

Practical and economic shortcomings

Given the practical and ideological obstacles to the introduction of input–output techniques in communist planning, the material balances system, which 'is not inherently wasteful or theoretically unsound',[1] was probably the only possible solution. Applied to foreign trade, it could be argued that, given the initial assumption of a basic tendency to autarky, it was a second-best approach. Demand factors, for instance, can be said to have been brought into the picture, since 'once certain domestic production and consumption goals were set, relative scarcities were indicated by the surplus of domestic demand over supply of the various goods in the material balances'.[2] Similarly, from the supply side, 'a strong comparative advantage was likely to show up as a surplus on the resources side of the material balance'.[3] But clearly such considerations can only partially justify a process which globally cannot lead to an optimum foreign trade programme. Consistency between import needs and export possibilities may be achieved, but there will be no necessary tendency for countries to specialize in producing those goods in which they enjoy a comparative advantage. In fact, as long as foreign trade is planned on a purely physical basis, without reference to domestic and foreign prices, the optimum position (for the world as a whole, and for the country in question as well, if it cannot influence the prices of traded commodities), in which domestic and world prices are equal, allowing for transport costs, will not be reached.[4]

Granted, therefore, that the material balances system cannot lead to an optimum, it leaves several further questions unanswered. For instance, how should trade, as determined by the material balances, be allocated between different partners, and how should countries select the industries which will be developed for export purposes?[5] In the case of a 'self-evident' comparative advantage, the answer to the second question may

---

[1] Montias, 'Planning with Material Balances', p. 974.
[2] Pryor, *Communist Foreign Trade System*, p. 100.
[3] Montias, *Central Planning in Poland*, pp. 167–8.
[4] P. A. Samuelson, 'The Gains from International Trade', in The American Economic Association, *Readings in the Theory of International Trade*, London 1950.
[5] E. Ames, 'International Trade without Markets—The Soviet Bloc Case', *The American Economic Review*, Vol. XLIV, No. 5, December 1954, p. 800.

be quite simply dictated by obvious factor-endowment considerations (e.g. timber or furs in Russia, coal in Poland, oil in Rumania). But what about more sophisticated manufactured products, for which only detailed cost comparisons can determine where an additional unit of investment will best be allocated to promote exports? A further problem, of an institutional nature, arises when major planning decisions, which are usually taken rather quickly, are co-ordinated with the signing of global trade contacts. As one Western author put this dilemma:

If a nation signs the global contracts before the material balances are balanced, it runs the risk of not filling some important import needs which are suddenly discovered, or of causing bottlenecks by contracting to export too much of a given good. If the domestic production plan is made first and the nation tries to fill the gaps in the plan (to equilibrate the unbalanced material balances) with imported materials and to pay for these with surplus goods, three dangers arise: it might get involved in some extremely unprofitable trade deals; it might not be able to obtain the needed imported goods after all, especially since some goods are in chronic scarcity on the 'Socialist world market'; it might be left with a surplus of unexportable and unusable goods.[1]

Minor criticisms can be made of the practice of selling different surpluses each year—this is unlikely to lead to stable commercial relations with the rest of the world or to the building up of a strong bargaining position. A further problem arises when one considers that the material balances elaborated in the various Gosplans cover a rather limited number of commodities. In Poland in 1956 these were about 1,500, but only about 200 were completely in the hands of the central planning agency.[2] According to a Russian source, 1,510 commodities were balanced by the Soviet Gosplan in 1960.[3] The estimates of Western authors vary between 800 and 1,600 (compared to only about 400 to 500 in pre-war days).[4] In Hungary, 400 to

---

[1] Pryor, *Communist Foreign Trade System*, p. 66.
[2] Montias, *Central Planning in Poland*, pp. 90–1.
[3] G. I. Grepsov and P. P. Karpov (eds.), *Material'nyie balansi v narodnokhozyaistvennom plane*, Moscow 1960, pp. 21–2.
[4] Levine, 'The Centralized Planning', pp. 89–90; Montias, 'Planning with Material Balances', p. 966; M. Dobb, *Soviet Economic Development since 1917*, 6th edition (revised), London 1966, p. 373; Treml, 'Input-Output Analysis and Soviet Planning', p. 107.

500 products, comprising about 50 per cent of national output, were balanced in central hands,[1] while in the DDR over 1,000 national material balances were planned at least during the First Five Year Plan.[2] Since all these material balances relate to the most important commodities, they are likely to include most imports assumed to be of top priority, but a good many exportable commodities may well never be considered, since they will be balanced only at lower administrative levels not directly concerned with foreign trade.

To sum up the main defects of the method: it ignores relative costs of production, alternative production processes and trade programmes and the relations between trade and investment.[3] Some of its most obvious defects are being rectified by the CMEA specialization agreements and long-term contracts, which introduce an element of long-run planning, and thereby encourage investment in sectors with a comparative advantage. At present, however, it remains one of the major instruments of foreign trade planning, both within each country and within CMEA. On the import side its importance is paramount; on the export side it is being supplemented (and at times replaced) by more refined calculations on the economic advantage of each single export.[4] But there does not seem to be, as yet, any real effort to abolish the method entirely and to go over to a price planning system, which would do away with the present emphasis on physical planning. This is shown by the use of the material balances techniques on an enlarged international scale, within CMEA, where almost exact replicas of national balances are being drawn up for commodities traded by the member countries.[5] Great use is also being made of them for perspective planning.[6] These methods, it is true, do show whether enough of any commodity is being produced by the bloc as a whole, and where surpluses and deficits arise but, as Soviet sources admit, they cannot, by themselves, indicate which will be the most efficient of the alternative patterns of specialization:

[1] Balassa, *The Hungarian Experience*, p. 63.
[2] Pryor, *Communist Foreign Trade System*, p. 57.
[3] Ibid. p. 100.
[4] See Chapter 5.
[5] M. C. Kaser, *Comecon*, pp. 36–8.
[6] B. Ladigin and Y. Shiraev, 'Voprosy sovershenstvovaniya ekonomicheskogo sotrudnichestva stran SEV', *Voprosy Ekonomiki*, No. 5, May 1966, p. 84.

With the help of the elaboration of combined material balances of outputs and demands for production for the whole socialist system (or for groups of countries belonging to it), one can establish approximate directions in the division of labour between countries, but one cannot as yet choose the most effective variant of specialization and co-operation. For this, one must find methods for determining the effectiveness of the Socialist international division of labour and elaborate a corresponding system of indices.[1]

[1] O. Bogomolov, 'O mezhdunarodnom sotsialisticheskom rasdelenya truda', *Mirovaiya Ekonomika i Mezhdunarodnoe Otnosheniya*, No. 4, April 1959, pp. 33–4.

5

THE EASTERN EUROPEAN
EXPERIENCE—'EFFICIENCY INDICES'
AND COMPARATIVE ADVANTAGE

The adaptation of the material balances system to foreign trade planning (as outlined in the previous chapter) may have been of some use in the Soviet Union, but its wholesale application in the early post-war years to the smaller Eastern European countries, whose dependence on international trade is much greater, was bound to lead them into serious difficulties. These came to a head by 1954–5. Up to that time the economic development of these countries had followed 'an indiscriminate imitation of the historically conditioned example of the Soviet Union',[1] so that heavy industry, engineering and, to a lesser extent, processing capacity were given top priority in planning. But the pace of their development quickly outran the increases in production of fuels, basic materials and agricultural output, and the consumer goods sector was largely neglected.[2] While Russia's sheer size, resource endowment and potential market vindicated, up to a point at least, an autarkic development programme, each of the much smaller Eastern European countries found itself developing huge steel mills or engineering industries out of all proportion to its domestic needs or export potential.

Between 1953 and 1956 several economic and political events (among them Stalin's death in 1953) precipitated the inevitable crisis engendered by this autarkic pattern. Soviet credits, which had helped Eastern Europe for a time, were exhausted, political relaxation permitted increases in consumption which raised import bills, shortages of raw materials and fuels became more pronounced and, since no new exports had been developed to

---

[1] V. Kaigl, 'International Division of Labour in the World Socialist System', *Czechoslovak Economic Papers*, No. 1, Prague 1959, p. 11.

[2] United Nations, Economic Commission for Europe, *Economic Bulletin for Europe*, Vol. XI, No. 1, June 1959, p. 39; and Vol. XVIII, No. 1, November 1966, p. 36.

take the place of non-priority traditional ones, the whole previously unbalanced growth path had to be drastically revised. In fact, planning for a minimum import content of national income, and exporting what was left over from domestic consumption, could not be a feasible policy for countries whose involvement in international trade (as measured by trade turnover *per capita*) was, before the war, between five to ten times larger than Russia's.[1] They now found themselves specializing in transformation industries for which no domestic raw material basis existed. And to purchase these materials from abroad they often exported in highly irrational ways, owing to the lack of foreign trade calculations. In Hungary, for instance, prune butter was produced for export, even though its production required a foreign exchange outlay that was in excess of the foreign exchange return.[2] Similarly uneconomic, and even less credible, given the size of the sectors involved, were Hungarian purchases abroad of iron and coke for steel production, when importing the steel directly would have cost less in foreign currency.[3] An analogous case seems to have existed for pig iron in East Germany.[4] In 1957 an official Hungarian document came to the conclusion that 'it is almost impossible to determine which foreign trade transaction is advantageous for us, and which is not'.[5]

Most of these blunders were due to the almost total neglect of foreign trade theory in the Eastern European countries. It was argued by Marxist theoreticians either that there was no justification for substituting a Ricardian scheme for a (practically non-existent) Marxist theory of foreign trade, or that socialist industrialization could not be achieved by following the principle of comparative costs, or that the international socialist market was, in any case, an 'organized' market to which these principles were not applicable.[6] Even stronger attacks on the

[1] F. L. Pryor, *Communist Foreign Trade System*, London 1963, p. 26.
[2] A. A. Brown, 'Centrally Planned Foreign Trade and Economic Efficiency', *The American Economist*, Vol. v, No. 2, November 1962, p. 17.
[3] Pryor, *Communist Foreign Trade System*, p. 28.   [4] Ibid.
[5] Quoted in A. A. Brown, 'Towards a Theory of Centrally Planned Foreign Trade', in A. A. Brown and E. Neuberger (eds.), *International Trade and Central Planning*, Berkeley and Los Angeles 1968, p. 65 (footnote 17).
[6] G. Göncöl, 'A propos de la théorie marxiste du commerce extérieur', translated from the Hungarian (*Közgazdasagi Szemle*, No. 11, 1955) in *Etudes Economiques*, Nos. 95–6, 1956, p. 89.

theory of comparative costs came from Russian sources.[1] But
the chaotic situation in so many of the Eastern European
countries prompted the recognition that 'an incorrect solution'[2]
had been attempted so far, and led to a theoretical rediscovery
of Ricardo with admissions such as that 'the economic returns
from foreign trade can be determined only by a comparison
of national and international values'.[3] As a result, the real
problem facing Eastern European economists became that of
measuring comparative costs and assessing where the comparative advantage of each country lay. The main difficulty was
(and is) that the two elements which intervene in such comparisons, the prices of individual commodities and the rate of
exchange, had little economic significance. The rate of exchange
in a centrally planned economy has been called by Western
writers 'irrational',[4] 'irrelevant',[5] 'artificial'[6] and 'unrealistic',[7]
while an Eastern writer defined it as just 'basically wrong'.[8] No
known principle lies at the basis of its determination, except that
it has generally been overvalued. It does not seem to be fixed so
as to equate the demand and supply of foreign currency, or to
achieve equilibrium in the balance of payments, nor does it seem
to rely on any estimate of purchasing-power parity. Apart from
some 'non-commercial' rates of exchange, used mainly for the
transactions of foreign tourists, non-official rates have been calculated in Poland, Hungary, Russia and the DDR on the basis of
purchasing-power parity estimations, but it is unknown to what
uses they have been put, since the official rates of exchange 'do
not reflect the purchasing power of their respective currencies'.[9]

[1] A. Frumkin, 'Nesostoyatelnost burzhuaznoi teorii vneshnyei torgovli', *Voprosy Ekonomiki*, No. 12, December 1959.
[2] V. Cerniansky, 'Problems of the Economic Efficiency of Foreign Trade', *Czechoslovak Economic Papers*, No. 1, Prague 1959, p. 114.
[3] T. Liska and A. Marias, 'Optimum Returns and International Division of Labour', translated excerpts from the Hungarian (*Közgazdasagi Szemle*, No. 1, 1954), in United Nations, Economic Commission for Europe, *Economic Survey of Europe in 1954*, Geneva 1955, p. 133.
[4] Brown, 'Centrally Planned Foreign Trade', p. 12.
[5] F. L. Pryor, 'Foreign Trade Theory in the Communist Bloc', *Soviet Studies*, Vol. xiv, No. 1, July 1962, p. 42.
[6] A. Nove and D. Donnelly, *Trade with Communist Countries*, London 1960, p. 23.
[7] United Nations, Economic Commission for Europe, *Economic Bulletin for Europe*, Vol. xi, No. 1, p. 70.
[8] S. Balaszy, 'Rational Foreign Trade Decisions in a Planned Economy on the basis of Correct Prices and Rates of Exchange', *Mimeo*, March 1965, p. 2.
[9] G. Kohlmey, *Der demokratische Weltmarkt*, Berlin 1956, p. 266.

As for prices, neither in the Soviet Union nor in the smaller countries do they reflect opportunity costs. Production costs, whether marginal or average, are only imperfectly incorporated in them and demand factors have almost no influence on them at all. They are fixed by the central authorities, sometimes for very long periods, for a variety of purposes. Prices of consumer goods are relatively high, since they are subject to a turnover tax set at widely differing rates.[1] Department 1 (or producers') goods are, on the other hand, kept artificially cheap, often with the help of subsidies. Prices for agricultural goods vary between those set on the peasants' free markets and those set by the state's purchasing agencies. In inter-industrial transactions different prices are fixed at the enterprise and at the industry level for the same commodity, with further variations in sectors where costs of production differ widely between plants.[2] Such a chaotic situation is hardly likely to lead to any kind of meaningful international price comparison.

Two lines of approach have been suggested to the solution of the comparative cost problem: one would tackle the price system directly, introducing into it some element of rationality by, for instance, setting price relatives in conformity with, or nearer to, world price levels; the other would avoid interfering with prices and would attempt to compare domestic costs directly with foreign prices, trying, if possible, to account for some of the irrationalities in costing procedure. Given a more rational solution along these lines to the foreign trade issue, a third problem would be that of finding out whether the comparative advantage pattern so determined would also be the one chosen in the long run. The question here has been one of finding ways to 'dynamize' one's comparative advantage, or at least of attempting to maximize one's foreign currency returns in the long run by suitable investment decisions, both at the domestic and at the intra-CMEA level.

[1] On average, however, the rate is high and of the order of at least 50 per cent of the final price; F. D. Holzman, 'The Ruble Exchange Rate and Soviet Foreign Trade Pricing Policies', *The American Economic Review*, Vol. LVIII, No. 4, September 1968, p. 806.

[2] M. Bornstein, 'The Soviet Price System', *The American Economic Review*, Vol. LII, No. 1, March 1962.

Price reforms and foreign trade

Attempts to interfere with the present price structure present serious problems, both theoretical and political. Since marginalism has been regarded as a non-Marxist concept, any attempt to introduce it into price setting has been almost automatically rejected for a long time. Its use has, therefore, been mainly restricted to shadow pricing. Nor would it seem likely that any price reform could do away with the traditional policy of keeping prices fixed for a number of years. Such a practice automatically distorts any price structure in time, even one which might have been rational at the outset, since productivity changes, technical progress (and also changes in tastes) rapidly alter the relative demand-and-supply conditions of various commodities.

Since a wholesale overhaul of the domestic price system seemed, and still seems, unlikely, Eastern European economists have tried to focus their reform plans on a limited field, more directly linked with international trade. The central idea, with many variations, has been that of linking domestic price structures to world market ones. The proposals have usually been limited either to traded goods, or to potentially tradeable ones, or else to raw materials. In Poland, for instance, it was advocated in 1956 that the relations between raw material prices should be patterned as far as possible on the structure of world prices.[1] The theoretical justification given for this proposal, which had a limited application, was that price relations on the capitalist markets 'reflect socially necessary costs to a greater extent than under (Polish) conditions'.[2] In practice the reason was that foreign prices represented marginal opportunity costs to Eastern European countries.[3] The new prices of raw materials, fixed on foreign prices, would then, together with wages and depreciation, form the basis of prices of semi-manufactures and manufactures, thereby introducing some rationale into the whole system.

A similar proposal was made in Hungary. It was agreed that

[1] A. Zauberman, 'The Criterion of Efficiency of Foreign Trade in Soviet-type Economies', *Economica*, Vol. xxxi, No. 121, February 1964, pp. 5–6; J. M. Montias, *Central Planning in Poland*, New Haven 1962, p. 279.

[2] S. Michotek, quoted in Montias, *Central Planning in Poland*, p. 280.

[3] P. J. D. Wiles, *The Political Economy of Communism*, Oxford 1962, p. 111.

PRICE REFORMS 67

the prices of all goods actually or potentially entering into foreign trade should fluctuate around the prices prevailing on the world market.[1] This would provide some of the flexibility needed for purposes of foreign trade policy and the proposal, though difficult to apply, is now again under serious discussion. In fact, all the price reforms undertaken, whether in the 1956–8 period or in more recent years (1959 in Hungary, 1959–64 in Czechoslovakia, 1962 in Poland, 1963 in Rumania, 1964 in the DDR),[2] always fell short of achieving real rationality. Such an outcome was partly due to the habit of considering them to be once-and-for-all reforms, and not allowing any further price changes after the initial overhaul had been completed. But more important in explaining their failures is the fact that price differentials, to be effective, have to be unusually large, since input decisions are not very sensitive to price changes for physical targets and output volumes are the yardsticks by which an enterprise's achievements are measured. Usually cost increases can be justified to the central planners, if it can be shown that only by paying higher wages or higher prices for some material could the prescribed output plan be fulfilled; even if prices are set along rational lines, their function as indices of alternatives may well be very limited as long as bonuses and incentives are based on physical and not on value calculations.

Thus, for a rational price structure to become effective, the first need is for a radical reform of the present planning system, with its strong bias towards target fulfilment, output achievements and physical allocations of many materials, irrespective of their prices. Once this has been achieved, prices set according to opportunity cost considerations could fulfil their role for both domestic and foreign trade purposes. Tackling the problem the other way round, i.e. rationalizing prices without giving the economy any incentive to respond to them, would not lead very far. Once the possibility of effective decentralized choices among alternative inputs is given, then basing domestic prices on foreign ones makes sense. Implicitly adopting such a possibility, A. Nagy presents a scheme in which domestic price ratios would be set between the limits of world market prices

[1] Zauberman, 'Criterion of Efficiency of Foreign Trade', p. 6.
[2] M. C. Kaser, Comecon (2nd edition), London 1967, p. 187.

5-2

on the one hand and domestic technical substitution ratios on the other.[1]

His argument runs as follows: assume the marginal technical substitution rate (MTS) between two inputs (A and B) to be $MTS = a/b$ (i.e. by replacing the quantity a of input A by the quantity b of input B, one remains on the same isoquant). The domestic price ratio is

$$P = \frac{pa}{pb}$$

while the foreign one is

$$Q = \frac{qa}{qb}$$

If one has $MTS < 1/Q$, then efficiency would require the use of A, since A is less expensive on the world market than a technologically equivalent amount of B. One should now set the domestic price ratio equal to the foreign one, i.e. have

$$MTS < \frac{1}{Q} = \frac{1}{P}$$

This would encourage the enterprise in question to use A and not B; it would not, however, encourage the importing agency to look for A on the world market. To achieve this, the domestic price ratio should deviate slightly from the world one and lie between the technical substitution ratio and the foreign price ratio

$$MTS < \frac{1}{P} < \frac{1}{Q}$$

This would provide incentives both to the producing enterprise to use A and to the importing organization to buy A abroad.

That such a solution is advantageous to the country in question can be seen by examining Figure 4 where the isoquant I shows the various combinations of inputs A and B necessary to produce a given quantity of good X. We can assume that, with no foreign trade, the country produces at point D, using relatively larger quantities of input A in relation to B than does the rest of the world, which is producing, assuming that it applies the same techniques, at point F, along its price line QQ. Following Nagy's suggestion, the new domestic price line should now be

[1] A. Nagy, quoted in Brown, 'Centrally Planned Foreign Trade', p. 15.

set between the old marginal technical substitution ratio at point D (measured by the domestic price line PP), and the foreign price line at F. The price line $P'P'$ which meets these requirements could be chosen. The most advantageous solution would now be to equate the marginal technical substitution rate and the new price line $P'P'$ so that production would take place at point E; the amount LM of input B could then be imported from abroad, while HG of A would be exported (along the foreign price line QQ). This would lead to the same output

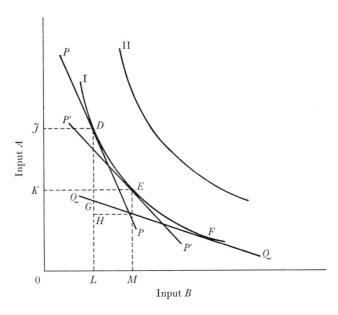

FIGURE 4

of good X, together with a saving of resources (equal to $JK - HG$) of input A. The argument, however, rests on the assumptions that the two inputs A and B are in fact tradeable and are not fixed factors of production, or labour, on which barriers to emigration may be placed.

However, Nagy does not seem to envisage such a possibility, since he aims at keeping the three ratios different from each other (i.e. $Q < P' < MTS$). Production is, therefore, going to be carried out either at the old point D or, at best, somewhere between D and E, or else, although this does not seem to be stated, on a new isoquant I', at a higher level of production. The necessary additional quantities of B could either, if supply is not inelastic, be found domestically at the new, and lower, price for B, or else be imported. In such a case the problem of how to pay for them is not solved, unless part of the increased output of X can be exported. Nagy's problem is really only that of finding some more adequate price structure, not that of both determining exports and imports and equilibrating their flows. Given this more limited aim his proposals have some value, provided that domestic price ratios, before the reform, are in fact completely irrational, so that any approximation to world market ones would be an improvement. But such an approximation would not necessarily lead to a better foreign trade structure. It would be possible, because of the irrationalities of price structures in centrally planned economies that, though $P > Q$, and therefore $P' > Q$, the 'real' price ratio should have been below Q so that, instead of importing B, the economy ought to be exporting it. P' will be a better price ratio from a domestic point of view since it will presumably shift production from the totally uneconomic point D but, in its foreign implications, P' may lead to a distortion of trade. Before the reform, assuming that prices were known to be irrational, the choice of which goods to trade may have been influenced by many considerations, not all of a price kind, and it is quite possible that B was exported. Now, however, as an approximation to a better price structure has been made, it can be assumed that B will be imported, since it seems to be cheaper abroad, and A will be exported.

Nagy's reform may be useful as a first step, especially as the case just outlined may not be too common, but it cannot take the place of a price system based on the precepts of classical price theory. This problem faces any reforms of the price mechanism in Eastern Europe—either they are not general enough, and by tinkering with one aspect of the question create new difficulties in other sectors or, if they are sufficiently widely based, they imply such large-scale organizational modifications as to be impractical. They may well be developed in the computing rooms and laboratories of research institutes or in the mathematical divisions of central planning bureaux, and be used there for linear programming models in a purely accounting function, but for such plans to be transformed into reality most of the existing economic structures would have to alter. The only other way, within the present framework, of achieving some rationality in foreign trade lies in a direct cost comparison, which avoids the problems posed by prices and the rate of exchange.

'Efficiency criteria'

The first suggestions along these lines again came from Hungary, in 1954: 'It is most economical to produce and export those products for which the biggest foreign exchange returns can be obtained per forint of wage-cost. On the other hand, in the case of those products for which this ratio is low, it is more economical to import than to produce them.'[1] These ideas were further formalized in Czechoslovakia, where the so-called export efficiency indices, which attempt to assess the gain from exporting certain commodities, were developed.[2] A large number of such indices have since come into use in practically all the Eastern European countries.[3] It would seem that only Albania has not followed developments in this field, while Rumania has now apparently caught up.[4] All the indices have in common some measurement of foreign currency earned per unit of domestic cost. The two most frequently used are

[1] Liska and Marias, 'Optimum Returns', p. 134.
[2] Cerniansky, 'Preisbasis'.
[3] R. Brauer, 'Zur Frage des Volkswirtschaftlichen Nutzeffekts des Aussenhandels', Wirtschaftswissenschaft, No. 3, March 1958; V. Shastitko, 'Metody opredelenya ekonomicheskoi effektivnosti vneshnyei torgovli v G. D. R.', Vneshnyaya Torgovlya, No. 1, January 1962; G. Shagalov, 'O metodach opredelenya ekonomicheskoi effektivnosti vneshnyei torgovli v Polshe', Vneshnyaya Torgovlya, No. 3, March 1962; A. Borisenko and V. Shastitko, 'Voprosy ekonomicheskoi effektivnosti vneshnyei torgovli v sotsialisticheskich stranach', Vneshnyaya Torgovlya, No. 5, May 1962; Z. Orlicek, 'Erfahrungen bei der Effektivitätsuntersuchung der Warenstruktur des tschechoslowakschen Aussenhandels', Der Aussenhandel, No. 11, November 1964. As for Western sources, see Pryor, Communist Foreign Trade System, pp. 106–14; Zauberman, 'Criterion of Efficiency of Foreign Trade'; J. Wilczynski, 'The Theory of Comparative Costs and Centrally Planned Economies', The Economic Journal, Vol. LXXV, No. 297, March 1965; United Nations, Economic Commission for Europe, 'Economic Planning in Europe', Economic Survey of Europe in 1962, Geneva 1965, Part II, Ch. 4, pp. 43–52.
[4] M. Kaser, Comecon, p. 191; G. L. Shagalov, Ekonomicheskaya effektivnost tovarnogo obmena mezhdu sotsialisticheskimi stranami, Moscow 1966, pp. 92–3.

the so-called 'global' and 'partial' indices. The 'global' index is:

$$E_n = \frac{C_d - M_d}{P_f - M_f}$$

where E_n is the index of export efficiency for commodity n, C_d is the domestic cost of production of a unit of the good, M_d the domestic cost of all the imported raw materials and semi-finished products used up in producing one unit of n, P_f is the world market price of the good (or the price it could fetch abroad) in foreign currency, and M_f the price of all the imports used up in the production of n (also expressed in foreign currency).[1] The 'partial' index is concerned only with stages of production and is of the form:

$$E_m = \frac{C_d - R_d}{P_f - R_f}$$

where R_d and R_f stand respectively for the cost (in domestic currency) and the price abroad (in foreign currency) of *all* the raw materials and semi-finished products used up in all stages of production *except* the last. For both the indices, the lower their value, the more profitable it should be to export the good in question. The partial index should also measure the profitability of each stage of production and show whether it pays more to export a commodity at an earlier or at a later stage of transformation.

Both these indices are at present in widespread use—by 1959 East German studies covered 70 to 80 per cent of all exports, while by 1961 calculations in Hungary had been applied to between 60 and 80 per cent of industrial products.[2] The indices are, however, open to several objections. The global one merely averages, over the various stages of production, the domestic cost of earning one dollar's worth of exports by individual export goods; should the export of machinery, for instance, turn out to be rather inefficient, because of the high cost of domestically produced inputs like steel, the global index would only show that exports of machinery should be curtailed,

---

[1] In Polish practice the terms M_d and M_f include not only imported inputs, but also exportable ones; M. Rakowski, *Efficiency of Investment in a Socialist Economy*, Oxford 1966, p. 255.

[2] Wilczynski, 'Theory of Comparative Costs', p. 78.

whereas it could well be economic to expand them by using imported steel.[1] The partial index is also open to criticism—e.g. the cost of manufacturing at the last stage of production may be quite low due to some technological innovation in the country in question; if, however, the commmodity is produced from very high cost domestic materials or from expensive imports it may be quite unprofitable, from an overall point of view, to go on expanding its production for export purposes.[2] In fact, both these indices can only give a first approximation to a solution to the problem, not a clear-cut answer.

Some other, even more obvious, defects are due to Eastern European practices in assessing costs. Only average costs of production are taken into consideration by cost accountants, and only average labour costs at that. This is due to the Eastern European interpretation of Marx, already mentioned above,[3] according to which there is no place for a rate of interest in a Socialist economy. Capital is therefore considered as a free good, the only exception being a depreciation charge, whose incidence, at first very low, has been recently increased. As a result costs include only wages, the costs of all material inputs (themselves cumulative labour costs) and an amortization charge, which is often too low. Apart from the absence of an interest rate, there is also no rent element for scarce resources. In practice, therefore, the foreign trade indices show the average cost of foreign currency per unit of labour spent. This costing procedure can lead in theory, and has probably led in practice, to some serious mistakes in foreign trade decisions. In the first place it is theoretically possible that pricing on the basis of average cost, instead of marginal cost, may result in a 'wrong' pattern of specialization and lead to the export of goods for which the country has no real comparative advantage.[4] Take the case of an economy with two commodities (a and b), both produced under conditions of increasing costs, though in industry B costs are rising less steeply than in industry A (cf. Figures 5 and 6). If we assume that the policy of maximizing

[1] Brown, 'Centrally Planned Foreign Trade', p. 19.
[2] Pryor, *Communist Foreign Trade System*, p. 111.
[3] See Chapter 1.
[4] Practical examples of the mistakes incurred in using average costs in foreign trade decisions are shown in A. Probst, 'Ob opredelenyi ekonomicheskogo effekta vneshnyei torgovli', *Planovoe Khozyaistvo*, No. 11, November 1965, pp. 40–3.

outputs at all costs does not lead to production being carried out at the technically most efficient point (i.e. where the marginal cost curve intersects the average cost curve from below), but at some point to the right of it (say at points Q and Q'), then pricing on the basis of marginal cost will differ

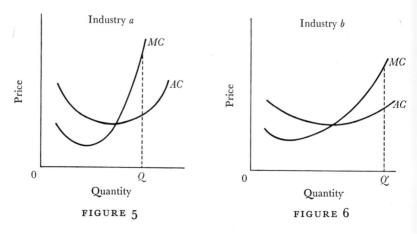

FIGURE 5   FIGURE 6

from pricing on the basis of average cost (assuming that any profit rates in excess of 'normal' profits are calculated at the same rate on both commodities). In fact, under marginal cost pricing we would have

$$\frac{pa}{pb} > 1$$

while under average cost pricing the inequality would be reversed

$$\frac{p'a}{p'b} < 1$$

If we assume that marginal cost pricing is followed abroad and that foreign price relatives are such that

$$\frac{pa}{pb} > \frac{qa}{qb} > 1 > \frac{p'a}{p'b}$$

then the practice of fixing the prices of the goods according to their average costs will lead our country into specializing in good a, in which returns to scale are quickly decreasing. Had it followed a policy of fixing prices on the basis of marginal costs, its comparative advantage would have been instead in good b.

A similar case can be made when, instead of considering two industries both subject to increasing costs, we take one producing under conditions of decreasing costs (cf. Figures 7 and 8). Here the price relations would be

$$\frac{pa}{pb} > \frac{p'a}{p'b}$$

with the first ratio standing for marginal cost prices and the second one for average cost prices. If price relatives abroad are such as to lead to

$$\frac{qa}{qb} > \frac{p'a}{p'b}$$

but

$$\frac{pa}{pb} > \frac{qa}{qb}$$

then our country, by following the average cost pricing principle, will find itself specializing in the production of commodity a, and not commodity b, where it enjoys increasing returns to scale.

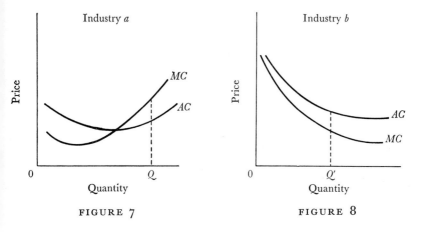

FIGURE 7   FIGURE 8

As for the lack of a capital charge, it would still be plausible either if capital were not scarce, or if it were immobile and could not be shifted from one use to another, i.e. if its marginal opportunity cost were zero. The former assumption is too unrealistic in the present stage of development of any economy, the latter would be valid only in the very short run if the capital was very specific. But in the longer run the lack of a capital charge creates all sorts of problems. Given two goods, A and B, if the export efficiency index for good A is lower than that for B, then A should be exported, provided however that its marginal capital–output ratio is also lower. But if B's marginal capital–output ratio is lower than A's, then the decision as what to export is ambiguous. With present practice A would be exported, and in fact the index gives a bias to the export of relatively capital-intensive goods (and to the import of relatively labour-intensive ones). Once again we have a case where the rules of comparative advantage may have been broken, even though the whole purpose of the indices is to apply them.

It has been officially recognized that the commodity composition of the Eastern European countries' foreign trade was biased in the past in favour of capital-intensive exports.[1] A Soviet study has even shown that the capital intensity of Soviet industrial exports was one-and-a-half times larger than the capital intensity of Soviet industrial imports (presumably, in fact, of import substitutes).[2] Thus a Leontief paradox in reverse could almost be applied to the Soviet Union. Leontief found for the United States that American exports tended to be more labour-intensive than import-competing production;[3] the empirical findings of the three Soviet economists apparently indicate exactly the opposite situation in Russia. Thus the United States turn out to be endowed with relatively more labour than capital, and the Soviet Union with relatively more capital than labour. But the Soviet example may not be quite as paradoxical as the American one. Firstly, the calculations apply only to industrial goods, and the introduction of the large volume of raw materials exported by Russia would probably transform the Soviet Union into a relatively labour-intensive exporter after all. And secondly, it is in the nature of the indices used in foreign trade planning to encourage capital-intensive exports. If foreign trade were based on price relations that

[1] M. Lesz, 'The Effectiveness of Investment and the Optimization of a Long-term Plan', translated from Polish (*Gospodarka Planowa*, No. 6, 1964) in *Mathematical Studies in Economics and Statistics in the USSR and Eastern Europe*, Vol. 1, No. 1, Fall 1964, pp. 45–6; G. L. Shagalov, *Ekonomicheskaya effektivnost...*, pp. 134–6.

[2] G. Smirnov, B. Zotov and G. Shagalov, 'Otzenka ekonomicheskoi effektivnosti vneshnyei torgovli', *Planovoe Khozyaistvo*, No. 8, August 1964, p. 29.

[3] W. Leontief, 'Domestic Production and Foreign Trade; the American Capital Position Re-examined', in R. E. Caves and H. G. Johnson (eds.), *Readings in International Economics*, London 1968.

reflected relative scarcities, the structure of Soviet foreign trade would probably be quite different.

It is true that ways out of the interest rate dilemma are being suggested and *de facto* interest rates have been introduced, sometimes for accounting purposes only, sometimes as actual charges paid by the enterprises for the capital they receive. By 1967 some type of capital charge had been adopted in wholesale pricing in all the Eastern European countries, except Rumania, and probably Albania.[1] This development is clearly making estimated costs more representative of the real costs incurred and makes the indices more useful in foreign trade decisions. New indicators have been suggested, which compare the foreign currency price with a 'full' cost of production, taking into account both direct and indirect labour *and* capital costs, and the use of input–output methods has been recommended to help determine such 'full' costs of production.[2] But the interest rates applied in such calculations are often determined on an *ad hoc* basis, without any attempt to set them at levels equilibrating the demand and supply for capital.

A further problem is presented by the pricing of the imported raw materials and semi-finished products used as inputs for export goods. At present the policy for such goods varies between, on the one hand, very high pricing, so as to discourage their use in favour of domestic substitutes and, on the other, the low pricing made inevitable by an overvalued currency. The former policy may well, for example, inhibit the use of imported oil in Poland, in favour of the consumption of potentially exportable coal. The latter policy, in contrast, encourages the lavish use of imports. Clearly the most rational way to account for the cost of imports is by estimating the cost of those goods which were exported to pay for the imports. This kind of opportunity-cost calculation does not, however, seem to be used in practice (though references to it have appeared),[3] since 'the

---

[1] Kaser, *Comecon*, p. 187.

[2] G. Shagalov, 'Voprosy ekonomicheskoi effektivnosti vneshnyei torgovli', *Vestnik Moskoskogo Universiteta*, Series VIII, No. 5, Sept.–Oct. 1963; and 'Ekonomicheskaya effektivnost venshnyei torgovli sotsialisticheskich stran', *Voprosy Ekonomiki*, No. 6, June 1965.

[3] E. Georgiev, 'Voprosy effektivnosti i rentabelnosti', *Vneshnyaya Torgovlya*, No. 7, July 1964, p 21; O. Bogomolov (ed.), *Ekonomicheskaya effektivnost mezhdunarodnogo sotsialisticheskogo rasdelenie truda*, Moscow 1965, p. 29.

advisability of imports is to a large extent predetermined by the needs of the national economy',[1] so that decisions both about the quantity of imports and about their domestic allocation usually ignore finer price and cost calculations.

On a macro-economic level imports are thus decided by the import plan, following mainly quantitative criteria. On a micro level the application of indices is probably non-existent at present, despite the frequently affirmed need for their calculation.[2] Theoretically their use could, however, help in decisions at the margin and in the choice between various commodities with similar uses. But once again, the irrationalities of the domestic price system bar the way to such applications. While it is up to a point meaningful to compare the price obtained on the world market for an exported commodity with the cost of production of this same commodity, it is much less reasonable either to relate the price paid abroad for a good to the arbitrarily determined domestic price of this imported good,[3] or to make use of the relation 'between the foreign currency expenditures on the import with the budgetary gain from the selling of the imported goods within the country'.[4] In the former case the decision would depend entirely on the arbitrary pricing policy adopted at home. In the latter it would depend both on the arbitrary domestic price and on an arbitrary rate of exchange. It could be argued that, if commodities similar to those imported are produced at home, then domestic costs of production can be compared to prices paid on the world market. Such a criterion would be similar to the one developed for export purposes, but would be even less precise, given the inevitable approximations which would have to be made in every case where the domestic commodity was only an imperfect substitute for the foreign one. Since the scope for import criteria, as noted above, is mainly limited to finer decisions at the margin, the rough and ready indices here suggested would be of very limited help in decision making.

Further defects of the indices involve their static character—

---

[1] E. Georgiev, 'Ekonomika sotsialisticheskoi vneshnyei torgovli', *Vneshnyaya Torgovlya*, No. 5, May 1963, p. 58.

[2] Shagalov, 'O metodach opredelenya...', p. 21, and 'Voprosy ekonomicheskoi effektivnosti...', p. 16; Georgiev, 'Ekonomika sotsialisticheskoi...', p. 58.

[3] Shagalov, 'O metodach opredelenya...', p. 21.

[4] Georgiev, 'Ekonomika sotsialisticheskoi...', p. 58.

they do not incorporate expected changes in world prices and are, therefore, valid only for the short run.[1] The limitations of domestic capacity and demand factors abroad are ignored, so that in practice perfectly elastic supply at home and perfectly elastic demand abroad are assumed. Thus a commodity with a very 'favourable' index may be exported, even though its domestic supply is very limited and recourse to similar imports may have to be made later in the planning period. Operationally the indices are often based on outdated information,[2] at times even give opposing solutions,[3] and (probably their most important defect) are not linked in any way to the enterprises' plans or bonuses. Thus producers are not interested in exporting, while foreign trade enterprises are only marginally interested in producers' costs.[4] In conclusion, the indices have, at best, enabled Eastern European planners to make reasonably rational choices between similar export commodities at any moment of time, but not to optimize a foreign trade plan.

Theoretically this is possible, on the assumption that there are no non-competing imports.[5] Suppose indices were calculated for all goods in the economy and were then ranked in a cardinal scale of profitability. The good which had the highest index would be chosen as the first import, the good with the lowest as the first export. As exports of this commodity increased, so too would its index, as two factors would alter—on the numerator side costs of production would rise relative to its price, on the denominator side the world price itself might decline as increasing quantities of the good were supplied. Conversely, the first import index will sooner or later decline, as either the cheaper sources of production abroad are exhausted, or prices abroad rise through rising costs of production

[1] Agoston, *Marché Commun Communiste*, p. 238.
[2] A. Nagy and T. Liptak, 'A short-run Optimization Model of Hungarian Cotton Fabric Exports', *Economics of Planning*, Vol. III, No. 2, September 1963, p. 119.
[3] United Nations, Economic Commission for Europe, 'Economic Planning in Europe', *Economic Survey of Europe in 1962*, Part II, Ch. IV, p. 47.
[4] S. Balaszy, 'Der Aussenhandel und die Reform der Wirtschaftsführung in der Ungarischen Volksrepublik', *Wirtschaftswissenschaft*, No. 11, November 1967, pp. 1877–8.
[5] A. E. Jasay, 'Criteria for Foreign Trading Decisions with Arbitrary Home Prices', *Mimeo*, July 1958; J. Pajestka, 'Certain Problems of "Profitability Calculations" in Foreign Trade', in J. Soldaczuk (ed.), *International Trade and Development: Theory and Policy*, Warsaw 1966, pp. 157–64.

or demand at home is satisfied at a given price. When the first export index reaches the value of the next lowest one, the new commodity concerned will also be exported, and so on. The same, in reverse, will happen for imports. This means that at the margin the two indices will be the same and will be rising (falling) together. Let E_a be the index for commodity A, increasing as a function of the quantity of A sold, i.e. $Ea = f(Q_a)$. We will then have:

$$\frac{dE_a}{dQ_a} = \frac{dE_b}{dQ_b} = \dots = \frac{dE_n}{dQ_n}$$

Equilibrium will be reached at a point on the scale where all the import efficiency indices have fallen to the value of the export efficiency indices. In such a case the ratio of domestic costs to foreign prices will be the same at the margin (a result which fits with the opportunity-cost version of the comparative advantage theory). The common value of the marginal index to which export indices rise and import indices fall could be considered as the equilibrium rate of exchange. The planning of foreign trade would then consist in a process of arbitrage between the two extremities of the scale, working towards the centre.[1]

The model, as described so far, neglects some practical difficulties. The indices may, for instance, fail to converge if increasing, or even constant returns to scale obtain in the domestic production of some export – in such a case the country would go on exporting just one product until it had become the world's sole seller or until its costs would be rising again. If the indices do not converge, movements along the scale will not provide sufficient indication of the desirable volume of international trade. In such a case imports would have to be limited to the volume of domestic consumption at an arbitrary domestic price, using the value of the index only to determine whether the good will be imported or not. Or prices could be flexible and vary as a function of the quantity of imports offered (or of the quantity of exports taken away from the home market). The further

---

[1] In a way this model, by not considering non-competing imports, is complementary to the material balances scheme (examined in the previous chapter) which, theoretically at least, attempts to fix an import plan only for goods not produced at home.

difficulty arising from the existence of non-competing imports, or of exports for which the country is a monopolist, could be overcome by placing the commodities in question at either end of the scale and importing (or exporting) until domestic and foreign demand are satisfied at equilibrium prices.

Though the practical difficulties of constructing indices for all commodities (at all stages of production), would make actual calculations impracticable, one of the basic ideas of the

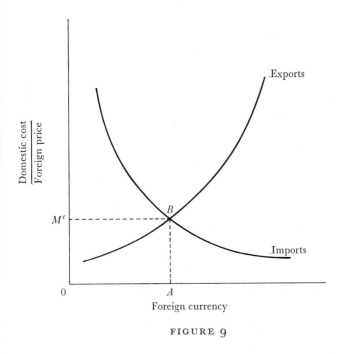

FIGURE 9

model, that of the equilibrium rate of exchange, has had some influence in Eastern European practice. This rate expresses the maximum amount of domestic currency that should be spent in earning one unit of foreign currency. In Figure 9 the equilibrium rate of exchange is determined by the intersection of the import and export curves, given by the previously outlined model, at point B and is equal, in foreign currency, to the amount $0A$. Above this rate, though a larger quantity of foreign exchange could be earned, the domestic cost incurred would

6

outweigh any benefits reaped from increased imports, while below this rate no further advantages could be obtained by expanding foreign trade. This very 'marginal' concept, called in Poland the 'limit rate of exchange', was first used in foreign trade planning in the middle of the 1960s and is slowly receiving wider application. So far it provides the only rational method of converting foreign into domestic prices. In a market economy, the rate of exchange has a wider function and is meant to express the marginal value of a unit of foreign currency in conditions in which this unit can be used for both capital and current (visible and invisible) transactions. In Eastern European countries, however, where trade accounts for the bulk of international transactions, the decision to limit the economic significance of the rate of exchange to the value of forgone imports can be regarded as relatively rational. The value of service items entering into the balance of payments is apparently very small,[1] while capital movements are almost non-existent, apart from aid, which is hardly influenced by exchange-rate considerations.[2]

The rate provides an absolute measure of the advantage of foreign trade, as opposed to the quotient-type criteria, since any export will be profitable whose foreign currency earnings (D), converted into domestic currency at the marginal rate of exchange (M^e), exceed the domestic costs of production (C)

$$M^e D > C$$

Similarly it provides a criterion for choosing between various commodities, as it can rank them in a cardinal order:

$$M^e D_1 - C_1 > M^e D_2 - C_2 > \ldots > M^e D_n - C_n$$

[1] In any case, one type of invisible transaction which has been growing rapidly in recent years, namely tourism, would require its own rate of exchange in view of the wide disparities between the wholesale price level, which is not subject to indirect taxation, and the retail price level, which bears all the incidence of turn-over taxes; O. Sik, *Plan and Market under Socialism*, Prague 1967, p. 327; P. J. D. Wiles, *Communist International Economics*, Oxford 1968, p. 140.

[2] Some idea of the relative importance of various international transactions for the Soviet Union can be found in: M. Caiola, 'Balance of Payments of the U.S.S.R., 1955–8', *International Monetary Fund Staff Papers*, Vol. IX, No. 1, March 1962, and 'Balance of Payments of the U.S.S.R., 1959–1960', *International Monetary Fund Staff Papers*, Vol. X, No. 2, July 1963, and for the DDR in H. Köhler, *Economic Integration in the Soviet Bloc: with an East German Case Study*, New York 1965, pp. 328–31.

and allows choices whenever two commodities sold on different markets have the same quotient index, should the marginal rates of exchange differ between currencies.

The use of the limit rate of exchange concept has been especially frequent in the foreign trade linear programming models recently developed in Eastern European countries.[1] But it has also been integrated into the more normal quotient- (or index-) type analysis of foreign trade efficiency and has added an extra degree of precision, by allowing not only a straightforward comparison of domestic and foreign costs and prices, but also a differentiation of foreign markets according to various marginal rates fixed, presumably, at the beginning of each planning period. New indices, incorporating this idea, have usually been expressed as follows[2]

$$E_k^r = \frac{C_k}{K^r d_k^r}$$

where C_k is the domestic full cost (inclusive therefore of some interest charge) and d_k^r the foreign price of commodity k on market r. K^r is the rate of 'directional effectiveness' of market r and expresses the ratio between the marginal rate for this market, M^r, and the marginal rate of the currency in terms of some basic foreign currency (as shown in Figure 9). If trade were free with all countries, there would be no need for a K^r ratio, since commodities would be automatically sold on those markets which were most profitable at a uniform rate of exchange. But given the practical conditions of Eastern European foreign trade, with its bilateral trade flows, state agreements, long-term planning, barriers to exports to the West and will to achieve balance of payments equilibria, different markets obtain different treatment and provide different economic effects. Thus, the higher is K^r, i.e. the higher the ratio between M^r and M^e, the more profitable it is to export to market r, even if it entails a larger outlay of domestic resources.

The index E_k^r represents perhaps the most sophisticated of all the indices so far used in foreign trade planning in Eastern

[1] W. Trzeciakowski, 'Model tekuschcei optimisatsyi vneshnyei torgovli i ee primenenie', *Vneshnyaya Torgovlya*, No. 6, June 1964; see also Chapter 6.
[2] Georgiev, 'Voprosy effektivnosti...', p. 23; United Nations, Economic Commission for Europe, 'Economic Planning in Europe', *Economic Survey of Europe in 1962*, Part II, Ch. 4, p. 52.

Europe. Apart from the usual classification of tradeable commodities according to profitablity, given by previous indices as well, it also provides directional differentiation between markets and gives a measure of the absolute gain, expressed in domestic currency, achieved by trading with each country or group of countries. It does not, however, take into account the problems posed by limited absorption power abroad (though yearly changes in the M^r's could give an indication of this), or by fixed capacities at home, nor does it as yet attempt to opitimize a foreign trade plan, as opposed to providing guidelines for relatively more rational decisions.

Investment planning and foreign trade

Even if the major defects of the more or less simple indices so far examined could be corrected, their static character does not provide for any projection into the future of the comparative advantage pattern outlined at any moment of time. Hence the increasing importance being given in Eastern European countries to the question of linking the older discussion on criteria for investments to the more recent one on criteria for foreign trade,[1] since quite often it is the external economic relations of the centrally planned economies which have the greatest impact on the profitability of their investments.[2] A relatively simple solution to the problem would be merely to 'dynamize' the present export efficiency indices by introducing into them, not present domestic costs and foreign prices, but the upper and lower limits of expected domestic costs (given assumptions about future investments and replacements) and expected prices abroad for some future period. The indices would then lie over a range and some overlapping would probably be inevitable. While such calculations would give some indication of the most profitable lines of specialization, provided reasonable estimates of future trends existed, they would not show which investment in which particular branch would be optimal.

[1] V. Terekhov and V. Shastitko, 'O metodike sravnenyi effektivnosti kapitalnich vlozhenyi v stranach-chlenach S.E.V.', *Planovoe Khozyaistvo*, No. 11, November 1961, pp. 78–86; Zauberman, 'Criterion of Efficiency of Foreign Trade', pp. 8–9, and 'The Soviet and Polish Quest for a Criterion of Investment Efficiency', *Economica*, Vol. XXIX, No. 115, August 1962.

[2] Agoston, *Marché Commun Communiste*, p. 241.

Exports from industries in which investments had been concentrated would, it is true, in all likelihood enjoy favourable indices, but there would be no assurance that the same investment funds allocated to some other sector would not have raised that sector's export efficiency (or for that matter import-replacing capacity) even further.

The real problem, therefore, is not so much to see in which industry, on the basis of present indicators, capacity should be expanded, as to estimate the likely foreign currency returns for each new investment in each alternative use. Such an issue is clearly related to the more general problem of investment criteria in Eastern European countries, a problem which so far has generated a good deal of discussion, but few acceptable conclusions. The main difficulty lies in the Marxist condemnation of the rate of interest, mentioned earlier, which has retarded and hampered the introduction of new ideas. By now the usefulness of an interest rate has been accepted more or less openly in all the Eastern European countries, with the possible exception of Albania, not only as an accounting device for the allocation of investment funds but even, at times, as an actual price for capital. The terminology used to define it, however, still pays lip service to ideology, and clouds the concept in formulations such as 'national average normative coefficient of the efficiency of capital investment'. Furthermore, its determination is more influenced by purely technological considerations on the micro-economic level and by *ad hoc* decisions of central planners on the macro level, than by the interplay of economic forces.

The best known, and also most widely applied, of such interest-rate-type criteria for investment is the Soviet 'recoupment period' idea, which enables a planner to choose between alternative projects having different capital outlays and current expenditure patterns. If project 1, for instance, requires a larger initial investment than project 2, but will save on current costs, project 1, will be preferred, provided that the gain in savings on current expenditure wipes out the extra investment required at the outset within a prescribed number of years—the recoupment period. Should the saving in current costs not be sufficient to outweigh the higher investments, within the prescribed period, then the more capital-intensive project will be chosen.

If I stands for the sum invested, C for the cost of production and T for the fixed recoupment period, then

$$\frac{I_1 - I_2}{C_2 - C_1} = T$$

or

$$\frac{1}{T} = \frac{C_2 - C_1}{I_1 - I_2}$$

and $1/T$ becomes a *de facto* interest rate.[1] But this method attempts to answer only the limited question of a choice between alternatives within a particular industry, since different recoupment periods (i.e. rates of interest), are set for different sectors. Clearly its applicability to investment related to foreign trade is limited. Little headway can be made in deciding which line it is most profitable to develop for export purposes, if one sector of the economy is charged a higher interest rate than another (even if the rate in question is only a shadow one). This may explain why Soviet economists stick to a differential rate of interest system, which they defend by arguing that vital sectors of the economy must be granted easier pay-off terms than less important sectors, since 'vital' and 'less important', at least for the Soviet Union, can be assessed in a purely autarkic way.[2] But for countries where production, investment and foreign trade decisions are as tightly linked to each other as is the case in the smaller and more foreign-trade-dependent countries of CMEA, the adoption of a unique value for the rate of interest would seem to be more sensible. While Poland and Hungary have in fact adopted single rates for the whole economy (15 per cent and 20 per cent respectively),[3] Czechoslovakia, Rumania and Bulgaria are so far following the Soviet example and applying different capital charges according to sectors.[4] But criticisms of this procedure have been voiced recently, even by Russian authors, who have recommended the adoption of a uniform rate, at least for foreign trade purposes.[5]

[1] A. Nove, *The Soviet Economy*, London 1961, pp. 211–12.
[2] Zauberman, 'The Soviet and Polish Quest', p. 237.
[3] Wilczynski, 'Theory of Comparative Costs', p. 75; Terekhov and Shastitko, 'O metodike sravnenyi', p. 81.
[4] T. Khachaturov, 'Opredelenye effektivnosti kapitalnich vlozhenyi v stranach S.E.V.', *Voprosy Ekonomiki*, No. 7, July 1964, pp. 130–7.
[5] Shagalov, *Ekonomicheskaya effektivnost tovarnogo*...p. 66.

More sophisticated attempts have been made to measure the incremental investment entailed in increasing export, or import-substituting, production, by a coefficient similar to a marginal capital–output ratio,[1] e.g.

$$IE = \frac{\Sigma(P_f - M_f)}{I_d}$$

where IE is the index of the foreign currency efficiency of investment, $\Sigma(P_f - M_f)$ the additional amount of foreign exchange obtained during a period (a year) as a result of the increased productive capacity of the export industry, and I_d the amount of investment necessary to ensure the planned increase in productive capacity, measured in domestic currency.[2] A similarly simple formulation relates foreign exchange receipts to both investments and current costs of production:

$$IE' = \frac{V_f}{C_d + Ki}$$

where V_f stands for the net foreign currency receipts from the export, C_d is the domestic cost of production, K is the capital investment per unit of export and i is the *de facto* rate of interest.[3] Both these can only be applied to investments which either have the same period of useful life (since they do not take into account the different patterns of gestation and fruition), or else have similar current costs. Neither is, therefore, much use in directing investment into the most profitable sectors. They can, at best, only help in the selection of alternatives for similar commodities.

The real need is for one unified criterion with universal applicability, which would enable the planners to decide between any investment in any sector, whether these investments have any direct relevance to foreign trade or not. The first attempt at such a formulation was made in Poland, and most of the economic calculations of the First and Second Five

---

[1] Zauberman, 'The Criterion of Efficiency of Foreign Trade...', p. 9.
[2] Wilczynski, 'Theory of Comparative Costs', p. 74.
[3] Borisenko and V. Shastitko, 'Voprosy ekonomicheskoi effektivnosti', p. 30.

Year Plans (1952–61) were based on it. The formula is as follows:[1]

$$IE'' = \frac{I + Iqn + \sum\limits_{1}^{n} K_i + \sum\limits_{1}^{n} R_i}{\sum\limits_{1}^{n} P_i}$$

where IE'' is the efficiency index to be minimized, I stands for the investment expenditure, q for the rate of interest applied, K_i for the yearly operating costs, R_i for the yearly maintenance and depreciation charges and P_i for the yearly output; n is the number of years for which the project is expected to be in operation. The formula was applied specifically to foreign trade by dividing the numerator by the net foreign currency yield of the project throughout its service life (instead of total output).[2] However, both variants ignored the time pattern of investment outlays, operating costs and output produced, for which the averages, as calculated by the above formula, are clearly unsuited. To take into account this further factor, a simple compound-interest-rate expression was introduced in the USSR,[3] so that 'the expenses incurred in later periods are brought into the present by being divided by a coefficient accounting for the average economic effect obtained by the productive utilization of the capital investment'.[4] This coefficient K is equal to $(1 + E)^t$, where E is the normative interest rate $(E = 1/T)$, and t is time.

Polish economists were more sophisticated and introduced a factor which took into account the 'freezing' of resources.[5] This factor (q_2) became, therefore, a measure of the national income derivable from a 'defrozen' unit of investment outlay. In practice it was fixed very near the actual rate of interest (or period of recoupment rate $1/T$) set for the whole economy. (There does not seem to be much reason, in fact, for the cost of capital to vary between the period of gestation and the actual life of

[1] Montias, *Central Planning in Poland*, p. 162.
[2] Montias, ibid. p. 166; S. Knisiak, 'The Economic Criteria of the International Specialization of Production in Socialist Countries', *Mimeo*, 1964.
[3] Zauberman, 'The Soviet and Polish Quest', p. 239.
[4] I. Shuckstal, 'Ob opredelenyi ekonomicheskoi effektivnosti kapitalnich vlozhenyi v stranach-chlenach S.E.V.', *Voprosy Ekonomiki*, No. 10, October 1961, p. 105.
[5] Zauberman, 'The Soviet and Polish Quest', p. 239.

the project.) The completed Polish formulation, since also adopted in Hungary, is as follows:[1]

$$IE''' = \frac{1/T \cdot I \cdot (1 + q_z n) + K}{P}$$

where $1/T$ is the national rate of interest, I the total investment outlay, n the construction period, or period of capital 'freeze', K the total operating costs and P the total output volume. The last two are sometimes adjusted by two further coefficients in more complicated expressions.[2] The foreign trade version of this formulation substitutes for P the net sum of foreign currency receipts yielded by the project.[3]

Theoretically these formulae seem quite satisfactory. Their main drawback lies in the use of inter-industrial prices for their calculation. These prices are known to be calculated net of interest rate charges and are often subject to large subsidies (though only seldom, at this level, to taxation). Thus some constant biases may be fed into the investment indices. In Poland: 'the acute shortage of foreign currency, for example, should have predisposed the planners towards technical processes which made more intensive use of domestic resources; but since the prices of imports did not reflect the real extent of their scarcity, investment calculations could not be expected to reveal the best alternatives'.[4] Only in Hungary does it seem that world market prices are used, at least for investment projects producing for exports.[5] The use of the current rate of exchange to translate these prices into forints does, however, limit the usefulness of the calculations,[6] and it may well be true, as has been argued, that both the 30 per cent devaluation of the Bulgarian lev in 1962 and the Soviet 1961 rouble reform had

[1] United Nations, Economic Commission for Europe, 'Economic Planning in Europe', *Economic Survey of Europe in 1962*, Part II, Ch. 4, p. 39.
[2] Zauberman, 'The Soviet and Polish Quest', p. 239.
[3] A. Nowicki, 'Premiers contours d'une théorie du commerce extérieur dans un pays à économie planifiée—le cas des échanges commerciaux de la Pologne', *Cahiers de l'I.S.E.A.*, Série G (No. 13), No. 124, April 1962, p. 199.
[4] Montias, *Central Planning in Poland*, p. 170.
[5] United Nations, Economic Commission for Europe, *Economic Survey of Europe in 1961*, Geneva 1962, Part I, p. 36.
[6] United Nations, Economic Commission for Europe, 'Economic Planning in Europe', *Economic Survey of Europe in 1962*, Part II, Ch. 4, p. 49.

among their aims that of facilitating comparisons between free market and domestic prices so as to help in the drawing up of investment criteria.[1]

Intra-CMEA specialization

The discussion of investment planning and foreign trade has been given a new twist in recent years as the CMEA commission has planned for a continuation of specialization within the area. The agreements of the 1950s on intra-bloc division of labour did not amount to much more than a rough and ready application of the Heckscher–Ohlin factor endowment criterion. Thus it was planned that Bulgaria would specialize in agricultural production among other things, Czechoslovakia in engineering goods, Rumania in oil, Russia in practically everything and Albania in practically nothing. Later on, as more rational planning methods were adopted domestically, the Commission tried to determine specialization patterns by allocating to countries the mass production of those commodities in which their export efficiency indicators were most favourable.[2] But even this policy, while it allowed for greater detail in intra-sectoral specialization, was not much more than a rationalization of the first method. Present studies, on the other hand, try to work out possible patterns of longer-run comparative advantage and the likely gains and losses accruing to each country from specialization. The theories and formulas that have been put forward are, as yet, few and relatively simple. This is understandable in view of the difficulties already encountered in constructing domestic efficiency indices; attempting inter-country comparisons greatly increases such problems.

One type of formula at present used by CMEA runs as follows:

$$T = \frac{\overset{t}{\Sigma} K_s P_s - \overset{p}{\Sigma} K_n P_n \pm DR_{ek}}{\underset{t}{\overset{p}{\Sigma}} S_n P_n - \overset{t}{\Sigma} S_s P_s \pm DR_{es}}$$

where K_s and K_n are the capital costs per unit of output before (n) and after (s) specialization, S_s and S_n the current costs, p the

[1] United Nations, Economic Commission for Europe, *Economic Survey of Europe in 1961*, Part I, p. 36.
[2] Kaser, *Comecon*, p. 192.

number of sectors before, and t the number after, specialization, D the balance of trade for all the sectors covered by the agreements, R_{ek} and R_{es} the average foreign currency efficiency indicators for investment and current expenditure respectively, and T the recoupment period.[1] It is argued that for specialization to be worth while the recoupment period (or interest rate) should be lower (higher) for the additional capital invested in the branches that have been chosen for specialization than for other domestic investment. From an examination of the expression it can be seen that it is no more than a simple adaptation of the very first type of investment planning criterion adopted in the Eastern European countries, which has been discussed above. The only difference is that it adds a foreign currency variable, as the aim of the index is not merely to save on current or capital resources, but also to improve the country's trade balance. The use of such a formula is, however, limited, since it applies to only one country and does not, therefore, allow a choice of projects between countries. An indirect solution to this problem would be feasible, if recoupment periods were to be calculated for each country and for each possible specialization pattern. The lowest ones would then be chosen. But even in such a case it will be impossible to assess the general economic effect of increased division of labour on all the member countries, even if allocative efficiency were improved.

A more general formulation allows some sort of comparison between countries of the economic effects of various policies. It takes the following form:

$$S = \frac{p_1 q_1 + p_2 q_2 - p_1' q_1' + [(q_1' - q_1)d_1 - q_2 d_2] \, k_r}{p_1 q_1 + p_2 q_2}$$

where p represents unit costs of production and q the quantity of output in sectors 1 and 2 before specialization; p_1' and q_1' are costs and output in sector 1 after complete specialization; d_1 is the foreign currency price obtained for product 1 abroad, d_2 the foreign currency price paid to obtain product 2 from the partner country which has followed the opposite specialization pattern, and k_r the marginal rate of exchange with that

[1] P. Glikman, 'Ob effektivnosti spetsialisatsyi i kooperirovanya proisvodstva stran chlenov SEV', *Voprosy Ekonomiki*, No. 2, February 1967.

country.[1] S is the total effect of specialization and, converted at some rate of exchange, can be compared with the S's of other countries. No explicit assurance is given that each country will benefit equally from division of labour and enjoy balance of trade equilibrium, but reshuffling between countries of various sectors could lead to some pattern of specialization which satisfied both efficiency and welfare considerations. Such a (nearly) optimal pattern is as yet very far from having been attained. The difficulties encountered by CMEA in its attempts at allocating different sectors and production lines to various countries have been highlighted by the Rumanian case. It is obvious that national and international interests will often clash when intra-area decisions have to be taken. So far the literature on the subject has not indicated very clearly which should be preferred. It might have been expected that the internationalist approach would obtain overwhelming support, in the non-Rumanian press at least, since, in line with comparative advantage, it attempts to optimize resource allocation but, surprisingly, the right of each country to stick to its own position and refuse proposals that may go against its welfare has been defended even in a Russian source.[2]

A further thorny problem relates to the interest rate that should be applied when estimating intra-area investment efficiency. Three alternatives are open: a unique rate for the whole area, different rates for each country, and rates that are the same for all countries but differ between sectors. The first alternative would be the most rational. The last, though not optimal, could at least lead to correct intra-sectoral choices. As for the second, it seems *prima facie* to leave the door open for all possible types of planning errors. According to one Soviet source it has none the less been preferred.[3] If CMEA were a real customs union, with freedom of capital movement within the area, such a choice would automatically involve the flow of funds from the low- to the high-interest-rate countries and, were rates free to move, they would quickly be equalized by such shifts in demand and supply. Such a possibility does not exist

---

[1] A. Nowicki, 'L'intégration économique des pays de l'Europe Orientale', *Cahiers de l'I.S.E.A.*, Série G (No. 22), No. 168, December 1965; Rakowski, *Efficiency of Investment*, pp. 293–9.

[2] Shagalov, *Ekonomicheskaya effektivnost tovarnogo...*, pp. 20–1.

[3] Bogomolov (ed.), *Ekonomicheskaya effektivnost mezhdunarodnogo...*, pp. 143–8.

in CMEA, since capital movements hardly exist and interest rates are fixed centrally.[1] Having interest rates that differed among countries would therefore involve all kinds of distortions in investment planning, similar to what is happening already in the internal planning of those countries that have separate rates for different sectors. And it is difficult to see how, once it has been accepted that they can fix their interest rates as they wish, countries can be forbidden to alter them so as to obtain cost comparisons that favour them. If all the CMEA members, for instance, preferred to develop their capital-intensive production, they would all attempt to minimize the interest cost of their investment in this branch so as to underbid partner countries. Three outcomes would be possible: either all countries would reduce their interest rates to zero, or to some common minimum, or some countries would not go the whole way and a pattern of different rates would be maintained. In the first two cases the final decision would favour the country with the highest level of productivity, and this result would be achieved because rates had been equalized. In the third case, where competitive bidding stops before this result is achieved, the final decision might fail to be rational and specialization in production might be allocated to a country solely because the latter had been able to underestimate its real costs. Once again, the arbitrary setting of factor returns may stand in the way of rational resource allocation.

The main conclusion of this chapter, and it is not a very startling one, is that at the root of all the foreign trade problems of the Eastern European countries lies their irrational price system, which not only makes straight price comparisons and calculations impossible, but also infiltrates all attempts at 'purified' indices based only on costs, or at investment calculations which include a rate of interest. Short of a total reform of both pricing and planning policies, which would make prices flexible in the short run and responsive to scarcity and demand conditions, there seems to be little hope for the introduction of

---

[1] Some capital flows do in fact take place, and their level has lately increased as the Soviet Union has obtained foreign credits to develop its raw material resources for the benefit of the whole area. But the interest rates charged on such flows have been very low, only 2 per cent, though in shadow price calculations their efficiency has been valued at a 15 per cent shadow rate. Ibid. pp. 172–82; Shagalov, *Ekonomicheskaya effektivnost tovarnogo...*, pp. 178–83.

rationality in the foreign trade field. The Sik reforms in Czecho-slovakia, already mentioned above,[1] are too recent to be judged as yet and their future is, in any case, very uncertain. They may well be on the right lines in so far as they will lead to a more direct contact between foreign and domestic enterprises and induce greater responsiveness to price changes in the decision-making process at the micro level (both as to inputs and out-puts). The only alternative would be the adoption of a shadow price system in a gigantic linear programming model which would attempt to maximize foreign currency yields (or total output, for that matter).

[1] See Chapter 3.

6

RECENT DEVELOPMENTS—
LINEAR PROGRAMMING AND
OPTIMIZATION

The material balances method of foreign trade planning provides for a consistent, but very much sub-optimal, trade structure; the efficiency indicators examined in the previous chapter, while improving the commodity mix of foreign trade, are incapable of achieving consistency between export and import decisions. So much has been openly admitted by a Hungarian planning document submitted to the United Nations: 'A consistent plan cannot be built on the efficiency indicators since the pattern of exports–imports is determined by other economic factors as well'[1] (beside the simple ratio of a world price to domestic costs). For the range of application of the efficiency indicators to be increased, many other variables should be taken into account, e.g. 'They must take into consideration, first, all the relevant conditions obtaining in foreign trade (i.e. not only foreign prices, but also foreign supply and demand); second, all the relevant conditions obtaining in production (i.e. not only domestic costs, but also productive capacities and raw material resources); and, third, the treaty arrangements in foreign trade (convertible or inconvertible currency, multilateral or bilateral terms, etc.).'[2] Such complex requirements can hardly be met even by the most sophisticated indicators. Mathematical techniques, on the other hand, can be very helpful in devising models in which most of these factors are considered, and in which optimization criteria for foreign trade are worked out.

The study and application of such models, which usually take a linear programming form, has been growing rapidly over

[1] United Nations, *Planning for Economic Development*, New York 1965, Vol. II, Part II, p. 78.
[2] United Nations, Economic Commission for Europe, 'Economic Planning in Europe', *Economic Survey of Europe in 1962*, Geneva 1965, Part II, Ch. 4, p. 47.

the last few years in several Eastern European countries, as the importance of foreign trade for them has grown, as intra-CMEA division of labour has been furthered and as the complexity of export (and import) decisions has increased. Research on mathematical models began as early as 1960 in Hungary[1] and Poland,[2] and is continuing both there and in the DDR.[3] The greatest advances seem to have been made in the three above-mentioned countries, but work has also been pursued in Bulgaria,[4] in the Soviet Union[5] and in other planned economies.[6] Most of the models that have been constructed are of a short-run nature, attempting, that is, to optimize the present structure of foreign trade. A few long-run models have also been built, and will be discussed below, but both their sophistication and their applicability seem rather limited in comparison with the former type of models. Among these, the most important distinction is between those which are concerned with the optimal structure of exports, or of foreign trade as a whole, in terms of direction and/or commodity structure, and those concerned mainly with working out the optimal criteria for a sector of the economy only. (As has already been noted in the case of the efficiency criteria, and for similar reasons, much less work is done on imports.) Since many of the sector models have been based on the breakdown or on the sectoral application of more general models, these will be considered first, while the industrial and more practical small models will be examined later.

[1] S. Balaszy, 'Aktualnye voprosy opredelenya effektivnosti vneshnyei torgovli', *Planovoe Khozyaistvo*, No. 8, August 1962, p. 88.

[2] United Nations, Economic Commission for Europe, *Economic Survey 1962*, Part II, Ch. 4, pp. 47–8.

[3] G. Grote, 'Zur Anwendung mathematischer Methoden bei der Planung und Leitung des Aussenhandels', *Der Aussenhandel*, No. 3, March 1963, pp. 9–11.

[4] G. L. Shagalov, *Ekonomicheskaya effektivnost tovarnogo obmena mezhdu sotsialisticheskami stranami*, Moscow 1966, p. 191.

[5] B. S. Fomin, D. Z. Davidovich and B. I. Aleinikov, 'K analisu vneshnyei torgovli v optimalnom plane', *Ekonomika i Matematicheskyi Metody*, Vol. II, No. 5, September–October 1966.

[6] G. Otto, 'Internationale Konferenz über Fragen der Aussenhandelsrentabilität', *Der Aussenhandel*, No. 6, June 1964, p. 14.

Global models of foreign trade optimization

The first, and simpler, attempts at using mathematical models were concerned with optimizing only the regional distribution of foreign trade, given a certain volume of exports and imports laid down by the central plan. They hardly ever, therefore, attempted to alter domestic production. One very simple model, developed in Poland by Fiszel,[1] assumes from the start an already optimal commodity composition of both imports and exports and restricts its task to 'an optimum combination of the geographic distribution of foreign trade'.[2] Taking the export sector first, and given the foreign currency price abroad p_k^s, on each market s for each commodity exported k, the upper demand bounds in foreign countries π_k^{es}, and the total quantities available for export X_k, subject to the constraints:

$$\left. \begin{array}{l} 0 \leqslant x_k^s \leqslant \pi_k^{es} \\[2mm] \sum\limits_{s=1}^{m} x_k^s \leqslant X_k \end{array} \right\} \quad (k = 1, 2, ..., n; \ s = 1, 2, ..., m) \qquad \begin{array}{l} (1) \\[6mm] (2) \end{array}$$

(where x_k^s is the actual quantity of k exported to s), the model argues that optimization can be expressed either in terms of maximizing foreign currency returns

$$Z = \sum_{k=1}^{n} \sum_{s=1}^{m} x_k^s p_k^s = \text{max!} \qquad (3)$$

or in terms of minimizing domestic costs (i.e. achieving a given value of exports with a minimum outlay):

$$Z' = \sum_{k=1}^{n} \sum_{s=1}^{m} x_k^s c_k^s = \text{min!} \qquad (4)$$

where c_k^s are the domestic costs of producing a unit of k for the market s (if product specifications for different countries require different outlays). Let $Z = f(x)$ and $Z' = \phi(x)$; then the optimum solution will be

$$F(x) = \frac{\phi(x)}{f(x)} = \text{min!} \qquad (5)$$

[1] H. Fiszel, 'The Calculation of the Economic Efficiency of Foreign Trade', *On Political Economy and Econometrics—Essays in honour of Oskar Lange*, Warsaw 1964.
[2] Ibid. p. 105.

Planning should strive at minimizing the numerator, maximizing the denominator and, in fact, minimizing the effective rate of exchange (i.e. the ratio of domestic costs to foreign currency returns).

As for the import side, if we know demand for imports at home (y_k^s), their prices (q_k^s) and supply limitations abroad (π_k^{is}), subject to:

$$0 \leqslant y_k^s \leqslant \pi_k^{is} \qquad (6)$$

$$\sum_{s=1}^{m} y_k^s = R_k \qquad (7)$$

where R_k is the total-import-requirement vector, the optimal allocation will be achieved if foreign currency outlays are at a minimum

$$Z'' = \sum_{k=1}^{n} \sum_{s=1}^{m} y_k^s q_k^s = \text{min}! \qquad (8)$$

(Let $Z'' = f(y)$.)

So far the model has not linked up exports and imports, and has ignored the very real possibility of balance of payments constraints, which are always present in the mainly bilateral, and usually balanced, trade of Eastern European countries. If, therefore, S^s is the planned balance of trade with market s (in s's currency), given that we want to minimize $F(x)$ and $f(y)$, we now want to minimize their product as well. Thus, the final objective function is

$$g(x, y) = F(x)f(y) = \text{min}! \qquad (9)$$

subject to constraints (1), (2), (6), (7) and to

$$\sum_{k=1}^{n} x_k^s p_k^s - \sum_{k=1}^{n} y_k^s q_k^s = S^s. \qquad (10)$$

Should trade be fully balanced, i.e. exports equal imports, then: $\sum_{s=1}^{m} S^s = 0$, and expression (9) would reduce itself to

$$g(x, y) = \Sigma\Sigma x_k^s c_k^s = \text{min}! \qquad (9a)$$

(since $\qquad g(x, y) = \dfrac{\Sigma\Sigma x_k^s c_k^s}{\Sigma\Sigma x_k^s p_k^s} \Sigma\Sigma y_k^s q_k^s$

and $\qquad \Sigma\Sigma x_k^s p_k^s = \Sigma\Sigma y_k^s q_k^s$).

A very similar model has been worked out by Marton and Tardos in Hungary, and is also concerned with an optimal distribution of given commodity volumes of exports and imports between markets.[1] It differs from the Fiszel one in so far as it considers imports and exports simultaneously and not step by step, and in that its balance of trade constraint is expressed in terms of an upper and a lower level:

$$v^s \leqslant \sum_{k=1}^{n} x_k^s p_k^s - \sum_{k=1}^{n} y_k^s q_k^s \leqslant v'^s \qquad (11)$$

(where v^s and v'^s are the two bounds between which a balance of trade can move with any country). Its objective function is expressed merely in terms of foreign currency maximization. It avoids converting all foreign currencies by a uniform rate of exchange by making use of an import price index (q^s) of commodities not actually imported, which is used in estimating the value of currency surpluses arising in different markets (in the case of balance of trade deficits it would presumably measure the value of forgone imports). The form of the objective function is as follows:

$$\sum_{s=1}^{m} \frac{\sum\limits_{k=1}^{n} x_k^s p_k^s - \sum\limits_{k=1}^{n} y_k^s q_k^s}{q^s} = \text{max!} \qquad (12)$$

The fact that q^s seems to be calculated for each different foreign market shows the preoccupation Eastern European planners have with balancing accounts with all countries. It would have been thought that at least surpluses accruing in convertible currencies could be valued in terms of world prices so as not to necessitate individual price indices for each partner, but the aim of balanced trade, even with capitalist countries (or at best currency areas), apparently imposes the necessity of balance of trade constraint and of estimating the relative value of each individual currency.[2]

[1] A. Marton and M. Tardos, 'Short-run Optimization of the Commodity Pattern by Markets of Foreign Trade', *Economics of Planning*, Vol. IV, No. 2, 1964.
[2] A more complicated Polish model, planning the geographic pattern of foreign trade, makes use of the exchange rates of 'directional effectiveness' (see Chapter 5); cf. J. Glowacki, 'Optimizing the Direction of International Trade in a Planned Economy', *Economics of Planning*, Vol. VI, No. 1, 1966.

A more sophisticated East German model goes further and tries to estimate the economic effect of exports and imports.[1] It calls c'_k the economic effect of exports, obtained by subtracting the domestic cost of producing one unit of $k(c_k)$ from the foreign price received abroad. On the export side, it attempts to maximize this difference:

$$\sum_{s=1}^{m} \sum_{k=1}^{n} c'_k x^s_k = \text{max}! \qquad (13)$$

On the import side, it calls e'_k the economic effect of imports, obtained by subtracting the domestic price of import substitutes from the foreign currency costs of the import. It again maximizes this difference:

$$\sum_{s=1}^{m} \sum_{k=1}^{n} e'_k y^s_k = \text{max}! \qquad (14)$$

And the objective function for the whole model becomes:

$$\sum_{s=1}^{m} \sum_{k=1}^{n} c'_k x^s_k + \sum_{s=1}^{m} \sum_{k=1}^{n} e'_k y^s_k = \text{max}! \qquad (15)$$

subject to the usual balance of trade bounds, non-negative constraints to the variables and exhaustion of the given exportable and importable quantities.

The last model would seem to be indebted to the Trzeciakowski partial attempts at optimization examined in the last chapter ($\Sigma M^e D - C = \text{max}!$), where M^e is the marginal rate of exchange with the particular currency under consideration, D net foreign currency receipts and C domestic costs.[2] But while Trzeciakowski makes clear the significance of his marginal rate of exchange (as the number of units of domestic currency needed to acquire an extra unit of the currency of market s), of his net foreign currency receipts (as the foreign price received, minus the import content of the export) and of his domestic costs (as including all the labour spent on this

---

[1] G. Otto, 'Optimierung der territorialen Struktur des Aussenhandels', *Der Aussenhandel*, No. 3, March 1963 and No. 6, June 1963.

[2] W. Trzeciakowski, 'Model tekuschchei optimisatsyi vneshnyei torgovli i ee primenenie', *Vneshnyaya Torgovlya*, No. 6, June 1964, pp. 22–4; United Nations, Economic Commission for Europe, *Economic Survey 1962*, Part II, Ch. 4, pp 49–53; see also Chapter 5.

and on the previous stages of production), no such rate of exchange and cost/price calculations are specified by the DDR economist Otto, whose model is, therefore, not only unclear but possibly misleading. Use of the official rate of exchange and/or of present cost calculations can hardly lead to an optimum solution, and the further problem of pricing imports which are not produced at home is not solved. While the aim of assessing the global economic effects of specific trade policies by estimating the resulting savings in resources is far-reaching and will probably be pursued. Otto's model is at present still far from providing a satisfactory way of achieving it. An even vaguer formulation of the benefits from trade is given in a model constructed by three Soviet economists.[1] Their objective function attempts to maximize the 'effect to society' obtained through the domestic consumption of commodities. Foreign trade is one way in which these commodities can be 'produced'.

All the models so far considered are open to some general criticisms—either they take into account only the foreign currency side, and ignore domestic costs, or else the treatment of domestic costs or prices is unclear. None of them attempts to alter the present commodity structure of foreign trade.[2] Their use is thus very limited, since they can only optimize the regional distribution of a sub-optimal volume and composition of trade. An even more serious drawback is that the number of variables and constraints taken into account is so large that none of the computers at present available in Eastern Europe is capable of solving the problems they pose. Thus, while as intellectual exercises they may be fascinating, as practical criteria for trade they are almost useless.

Two more linear programming models, one Polish, one Hungarian, manage, however, to be both general and computable. They are also more sophisticated, and many present attempts at developing sectoral, or improving general, models in Eastern Europe are based on elaborations or on combinations of the two. The Polish model, developed by Trzeciakowski,

---

[1] Fomin, Davidovich and Aleinikov, 'K analisu vneshnyei torgovli'.
[2] This is not quite true of the model of Marton and Tardos ('Short-run Optimization', pp. 81–3), which admits to some minor changes in trade flows as long as the domestic production pattern is 'not fundamentally changed'.

starts with the familiar balance of trade constraints already seen.[1] It adds a condition satisfying total final domestic demand for all goods:

$$\sum_{j=1}^{t} a_{kj} z_j + \sum_{s=1}^{m} y_k^s - \sum_{s=1}^{n} x_k^s = P_k, \quad (j = 1, 2, \ldots, t) \quad (16)$$

where a_{kj} is the technological coefficient, j the number and z the level of productive activities $\left(\sum_{j=1}^{t} a_{kj} z_j\right.$ expresses, therefore, the final output of commodity k in physical units), and P_k final demand for consumption and investment purposes for commodity k. The boundary conditions are not expressed (as in the versions just described) in terms of total export or import volumes, but in terms of production volumes, i.e. production must be kept within the limits of productive capacity (while imports and exports, as usual, must not overstep the demand-and-supply limits). Given these constraints, the objective function is of the simple form

$$\sum_{j=1}^{t} c_j z_j = \text{min!} \quad (17)$$

i.e. the plan will be optimal if the outlay of labour necessary for its fulfilment is at a minimum level.

Like earlier global models, it cannot be computed in its present form. Either many of the variables must be aggregated or else an indirect approach to optimization must be attempted. Aggregation permits a solution of the problem, but the results obtained will have little practical value for operative decisions in foreign trade, since such items as productive capacities, costs of production, outputs, demand, etc. are always related to actual commodities and not to very aggregated commodity groups. A preferable solution would therefore be to separate the original model into a set of sectoral programmes. It has been

[1] W. Trzeciakowski, comments in O. Lukacs (ed.), *Input-Output Tables—Their Compilation and Use*, Budapest 1962; J. Mycielski, K. Rey and W. Trzeciakowski, 'Decomposition and Optimization of Short-run Planning in a Planned Economy' in T. Barna (ed.), *Structural Interdependence and Economic Development*, London 1963; W. Trzeciakowski, 'Die Kriterien der aktuellen Effektivität des Aussenhandels und die Planung', *Der Aussenhandel*, No. 3, March 1964, and No. 4, April 1964; and 'Model tekuschchei optimisatsyi'; United Nations, Economic Commission for Europe, *Economic Survey 1962*, Part II, Ch. 4, pp. 47–55.

proved that the optimization of (17) can be reduced to optimizing partial problems on the basis of a set of constraints, once some subset of productive activities z_j $(j = 1, 2, \ldots, \alpha)$, domestic demand P_k $(k = 1, 2, \ldots, \beta)$ and traded commodities x_k^s, y_k^s $(k = 1, 2, \ldots, \beta)$ $(s = 1, 2, \ldots, m)$, has been chosen.[1] The necessary constraints are as follows:

$$\sum_{j=1}^{\alpha} a_{kj} z_j + \sum_{s=1}^{m} y_k^s - \sum_{s=1}^{m} x_k^s = P_k - \sum_{j=\alpha+1}^{t} a_{kj} z_j^0 \qquad (18)$$

$$0 \leqslant z_j \leqslant b_j \qquad (19)$$

$$0 \leqslant x_k^s \leqslant \pi_k^{es} \qquad (20)$$

$$0 \leqslant y_k^s \leqslant \pi_k^{is} \qquad (21)$$

where z_j^0 are activities in the rest of the economy and b_j is the upper production limit for activity j. The objective function will now be:

$$\sum_{s=1}^{m} M^e \sum_{k=1}^{\beta} (x_k^s p_k^s - y_k^s q_k^s) - \sum_{j=1}^{\alpha} \left(c_j - \sum_{k=\beta+1}^{n} l_k a_{kj} \right) z_j = \max! \qquad (22)$$

where M^e is the marginal rate of exchange and l_k the shadow price of commodity k. The former is a parameter obtained from the general model (as the shadow price of the balance of trade constraints), which is transmitted to the sectors. The shadow prices are obtained by solving the dual of the output-maximizing problems of each sector. Thus the task of the central planners is that of finding the value of the parameters (i.e. the M^e's) and, additionally, of feeding into each new sectoral problem the shadow prices obtained in solving that of the previous sector. That is, taking a different set or subset of activities each time, the (18) to (22) problem is solved for each of them; values of z_j, x_k^s, y_k^s and l_k are obtained and these are used for the next problem. The set of M^e's is centrally changed each time so as to ensure the equilibrium of condition (11). The process ceases when iterations do not give any more significant changes in the values of the variables and of the shadow prices.

Apart from the difficulty of knowing whether and when the iteration process will converge (though a Western economist has provided a slightly different method for the same model

---

[1] Mycielski, Rey and Trzeciakowski, *Decomposition and Optimization*, pp. 31–6.

which makes convergence more rapid),[1] a knowledge of the
c_j coefficients is needed for the model to work. These express
full labour costs at all stages of production (and therefore
require well-developed input–output tables).[2] At the same
time, they are net of amortization costs, since it is argued that
the very-short-run nature of the model does not allow for
investment planning, but only for an optimal allocation of
already existing capacities. Given its restricted aims: 'to
determine the volume of production of the separate exportable
commodities and of foreign trade, so as to satisfy the demand
for them set out in the plan, with minimal outlays of social
labour',[3] the model is both computable and able to optimize
short-run foreign trade.

An even more general model, less oriented towards foreign
trade and in fact applicable to the autarkic planning system of
a closed economy, as well as to the highly trade-dependent
Hungarian economy, is the so-called 'two-level planning'
model worked out by Kornai and Liptak.[4] The aim of their
model is to split the economy into a centre and a number of
sectors, since a global, centralized and, at the same time
sufficiently detailed model would not be computable. The
centre has at its disposal all the economy's resources and, on
the basis of the planned targets (determined by, for instance,
traditional methods), issues output and input directives to the

---

[1] T. Kronsjö, 'Iterative Pricing for Planning Foreign Trade', *Economics of Planning*,
Vol. III, No. 1, April 1963.

[2] A Russian introduction to the Trzeciakowski article ('Model tekuschchei
optimisatsyi', p. 20) expresses doubts as to the feasibility of finding (and, therefore, using) such 'full' labour costs, but the state of development of input–output
techniques in Eastern Europe does not warrant such a pessimistic conclusion. In
all of the centrally planned economies input–output tables have been developed
and perfected since at least 1958 (cf. J. Serck-Hanssen, 'Input-Output Tables in
the U.S.S.R. and Eastern Europe', *Øst-Økonomi*, No. 2, July 1962; L. Rychetnik,
'Mathematical Economics in Czechoslovakia', *Economics of Planning*, Vol. IV,
No. 1, 1964; M. K. Chaudhuri, 'Problems of Perspective Planning in the German Democratic Republic', *Economics of Planning*, Vol. IV, No. 2, 1964; V. G.
Treml, 'Input-Output Analysis and Soviet Planning', in J. P. Hardt et al. (eds.),
Mathematics and Computers in Soviet Economic Planning, New Haven 1967, p. 97;
and the Russians themselves have expressed the possibility of measuring full
labour costs by input–output tables; A. Zauberman, 'A note on the Soviet
Inter-Industry Labour Input Balance', *Soviet Studies*, Vol. XV, No. 1, July 1963.

[3] Trzeciakowski, 'Model tekuschchei optimisatsyi', p. 21.

[4] J. Kornai, 'Mathematical Programming of Long-term Plans in Hungary',
Mimeo, June 1963; and 'Two-level Planning', *Mimeo*, May 1964; J. Kornai and
T. Liptak, 'Two-level Planning', *Econometrica*, Vol. XXXIII, No. 1, January 1965.

economy's branches. Thus a supply assignment is passed down by the centre to the sectors and the availability of materials and a manpower fund for each sector are determined at the same time. These directives are the variables of the central programme. Its constraints will be the final consumption of each type of commodity and the total labour force available during the period. The sector's variables will be its productive, investment, import and export activities. Each sector will attempt to maximize its own foreign currency returns. Such returns are zero for productive and investment activities (unless non-competitive imports are required), positive for export activities and negative for import and import-competing ones. The central programme attempts to maximize the sum of all the sectors' objective functions: 'that central programme is regarded as optimal under which the sum of the maximal values of the sectoral objective functions is maximal'.[1]

So far the model follows quite closely Soviet-type planning practice. Its originality lies in the type of solution devised which is a mixture of competition and centralization. Each sector, given its directives (i.e. constraints) and its objective function, works out the dual of its own programme and thus finds out the shadow prices of the constraints. These shadow prices indicate by how much the foreign currency returns of the ith sector, producing the jth commodity, would rise if one more unit of capital or of labour or of a raw material were to be made available to the sector. They can be regarded as calculative interest, wage, rent, etc. Once the centre has allocated its resources to the sectors at the prices declared by them, it will expect them to work without a loss. Should a sector have announced too high a shadow price, and therefore be making an accounting loss, it will have to cut down its price in the next period and resources will be shifted to another sector. Thus the process is two-way: directives go from centre to sectors, shadow prices flow from sectors to centre.

The use of shadow prices here is slightly different from that implicit in the Lange–Lerner model, where the centre itself fixes the prices of capital goods and, observing shortages and surpluses, alters them until equilibrium is reached. For Kornai and Liptak resource allocation and target setting are fixed

[1] Kornai and Liptak, 'Two-level Planning', p. 160.

centrally while price determination is decentralized, as sectors try to carry out objectives and report back to the centre by means of shadow prices.[1] During the iteration process the shadow prices of the factors are equalized, i.e. the marginal returns of the resources are the same in each field of utilization. Kornai and Liptak argue that use of the maximization of the foreign trade balance as an objective function is little more than an illustration since other criteria, such as the minimization of total manpower expenditure or the maximization of external consumption, could be adopted instead.[2] But, as seen here, the aim of the model is not the achievement of a Paretian optimum in a Lange–Lerner type of economy, but rather yet another attempt to remove the one crucial bottleneck, namely shortage of foreign currency. However, it would not seem to be sufficiently general for this purpose. What, for instance, would happen to sectors which do not enter into foreign trade? Would they be left as non-priority sectors, with resources allocated to them after all the other sectors had been satisfied at the shadow price levels elaborated by them? Or would a second shadow price system be constructed for non-export sectors? Perhaps in Hungary all sectors are directly or indirectly linked to foreign trade, but in other countries this may not be the case.

But both the Trzeciakowski and the Kornai–Liptak models are global models attempting to optimize not just regional, but also commodity, structures of foreign trade and providing a method of solution. The first model is purely short-run, the second could also be used for long-run purposes, since it considers investment activities. Both adopt a mixture of centralization and decentralization (or decomposition), to avoid the dangers of excessive aggregation. For Trzeciakowski the centre fixes some of the shadow prices (for instance the marginal rates of exchange), and then uses them as parameters to influence sectoral solutions. In the Kornai–Liptak model the sectors work out the shadow prices while the centre only allocates inputs on the resulting basis. For Trzeciakowski the problem is that of finding a short-run optimum, given existing raw material and capacity limitations and the final consumption

[1] A. Bergson, 'Market Socialism Revisited', *The Journal of Political Economy*, Vol. LXXV, No. 5, October 1967, p. 664.
[2] Kornai and Liptak, 'Two-level Planning', pp. 166–7.

and investment demand determined by the planning agency. Kornai and Liptak, instead of taking planning as given and then determining foreign trade efficiency, start from planning itself and, by the way, also reach a foreign trade optimum.

Sectoral models

From the standpoint of both economics and computational techniques, the two last models are much sounder and more interesting than the others so far considered. But the number of iterations they require to achieve a reasonable degree of consistency may still be too high for them to have much practical importance. So, while computing techniques and new models are being evolved in the Eastern European economies, more limited and less ambitious sectoral models are being elaborated, and quite often applied, with positive results. Two very simple models, concerned only with exports, have been worked out in the DDR.[1] They are not really very different from the $\Sigma M^e D - C = $ max! models of Trzeciakowski, with the usual constraints and with slightly less refined M and C formulations. On similar lines is a model built to optimize the exports of Hungarian cotton fabrics.[2] The variables of the model are the physical quantities of cotton textiles exported to the various markets, where both actual and potential markets are taken into account. 120 articles, or groups of articles, and 67 markets are considered. The assumption is that each product is actually exported to 4, 5 or 6 markets out of a possible 10. The number of variables is, therefore, at most 1,200. The constraints are, on the one hand, the capacity limitations for each product and, on the other, the limitations of demand on the various foreign markets. These can take the form of upper limits, both in value and physical terms, or the form of fixed quotas to be exported to other socialist countries under some bilateral agreement.

[1] K. Gollmer, 'Optimierung der Exportrentabilität', *Der Aussenhandel*, No. 6, June 1963; K. von Krepl and K. Gollmer, 'Erfahrungen des A.H.U. Invest Export bei der Optimierung zusammenhängender Warengruppen des Maschinenbaus', *Der Aussenhandel*, No. 6, June 1965.
[2] A. Nagy, 'Un modèle d'optimisation à court terme des exportations et son application', *Economie Appliquée*, Tome xvi, No. 3, 1963; A. Nagy and T. Liptak, 'A Short-run Optimization Model of Hungarian Cotton Fabric Exports', *Economics of Planning*, Vol. iii, No. 2, September 1963.

The objective function should, ideally, be of the form:

$$H^{M^e} = P - (Q - R^{M^e}) = D - R^{M^e} = \text{max}! \qquad (23)$$

where P is the total foreign currency revenue of the exports, Q the total foreign currency expenditure of the programme (i.e. the value of total imports necessary for the exports) and R total domestic expenditure (thus $D = P - Q$). But it was held that in practice differences in domestic expenditure are negligible and that, in view of Hungary's balance of payments difficulties, a more simplified aim should be adopted, namely that of increasing foreign currency returns. 'This opinion is generally substantiated by contending that the testing methods at present used do not in fact permit a suitably precise estimation of how great the individual expenditures on the various products would be in the case of production patterns differing substantially from those now in force.'[1] In such a case, the objective function would be reduced to the maximization of the item D and all the M^e's would become zero. In practice it was argued that the expression (23) should be maximized subject to the use of varying M^e's. At one extreme, one would have $M^e = 0$ and the optimum programme would be the one maximizing only net foreign currency returns. As M^e was changed the value of the function H^{M^e} would alter and different programmes would be prescribed. The exact determination of M^e involves great difficulties at a sectoral level and cannot be satisfactorily achieved as part of an investigation concerned with the exports of a single industry. While a unique value of M^e cannot therefore be discovered, the use of several is quite legitimate and, by the adoption of this type of parametric programming, changes in the optimal programme could be examined. By computing the optimal programmes belonging to various rates of exchange, one can find out for what characteristic values of M^e the programme will change, establish by how much net foreign currency revenues alter as M^e is altered (i.e. as efficiency limits are changed), and discover the maximum amount of foreign currency available if $M^e = 0$ and if, therefore, the capacity in the cotton industry available for exports is fully used irrespective of domestic costs.

[1] Nagy and Liptak, 'Short-run Optimization Model', p. 128.

A slightly different approach has been developed by Otto, who has broken down his more general model into a sectoral one, again optimizing the territorial structure of imports and exports.[1] He has started from the situation of most Eastern European countries forced to have small upper and lower bounds to balances of trade with other socialist countries, but free, within certain limits, to accumulate surpluses with capitalist countries, whose currencies are convertible. Thus his objective function is limited to the maximization of foreign currency returns in terms of the capitalist markets alone:

$$\sum_{k=1}^{n} x_k^{m+1} p_k^{m+1} - \sum_{k=1}^{n} y_k^{m+1} q_k^{m+1} = \max! \qquad (24)$$

where $m + 1$ is the global Western market. While this apparently fits in with one of the most important present preoccupations of the centrally planned economies—that of securing as large as possible a surplus of convertible currencies to satisfy growing import needs—it led, when computed, to some unfortunate results.[2] Practice showed that the limits to exports to the capitalist world were provided not so much by the upper and lower limits of the balances of trade with the socialist countries, as by the demand limitations on the $m + 1$ markets. Thus the result was a marked improvement on the convertible currencies account, but a deterioration in all the other markets, compared to the initial situation. This result was possible because, with the socialist markets, the balance of trade was always kept at the lowest possible limit v^s, so that on each of them a deficit was created. A further defect of the model was that it did not attempt to optimize the geographical structure of exports to the markets from 1 to m.

Thus, Otto was forced to return to the more usual models, which attempt to optimize the foreign currency returns from all markets. But he makes an interesting point by stating that, in such cases, exports to capitalist countries would need some artificial stimulus (i.e. subsidy), since prices on the world market are usually lower than prices on the socialist market

[1] Otto, 'Optimierung der territorialen Struktur', June 1963.
[2] Otto, 'Probleme der Linearen Optimierung in der Aussenhandelspraxis', *Der Aussenhandel*, No. 3, March 1964.

(presumably this applies to manufactures, which are the DDR's main exports). Thus, unless a correcting coefficient d were applied, the inverse result to that of (24) would be obtained. The revised objective function becomes

$$\sum_{k=1}^{n} \sum_{s=1}^{m} x_k^s p_k^s + \sum_{k=1}^{n} dx_k^{m+1} p_k^{m+1}$$

$$- \left(\sum_{k=1}^{n} \sum_{s=1}^{m} y_k^s q_k^s + \sum_{k=1}^{n} dy_k^{m+1} q_k^{m+1} \right) = \text{max!} \quad (25)$$

Unfortunately, the author adds, such coefficients have not, so far, been estimated (nor would they seem easy to define without a good deal of arbitrariness being introduced into the calculations).

Long-term planning models

Linear programming models applied to long-term planning are even more interesting, since they would optimize the structure of foreign trade over time and, therefore, provide for some type of specialization criteria, a problem completely untouched on by all the short-run models so far considered. This is well recognized in Eastern European countries,[1] but, on the other hand, the techniques of long-term programming are much less developed and the number of unknowns, when considering foreign trade over time, increases very rapidly. Thus, some of the suggestions made for foreign-trade perspective planning remain on a very general and sketchy level. The rate of growth of imports can be extrapolated from past figures, if no large structural changes are envisaged; however, should proportions change, then imports may have to increase sharply (input–output tables could help in solving such a problem) and exports will have to be planned so as to equal, year by year, imports at their higher level.[2] This sounds more like a truism than like a long-run planning model for exports.

The Kornai–Liptak model, discussed above, can be adapted to long- (or at least medium-) term planning if the directives

---

[1] D. Schulmeister, 'Zur Optimierung der Waren- und Regional-Struktur im Aussenhandel der D.D.R.', *Der Aussenhandel*, No. 6, June 1965.

[2] G. Cukor, 'Use of Input-Output Tables in Long-term Planning of the Relations between Industry and Foreign Trade', in O. Lukacs (ed.), *Input Output Tables*.

given by the centre to the sectors are phrased in terms of both current, yearly flows of resources, including investment funds, and a final supply assignment for period $t+n$. In such a case, the optimal foreign trade structure for period $t+n$ will also be worked out, given that the objective function still prescribes sectoral maxima of net foreign currency revenues. It will be up to sectors (just as in the short-term model) to assess world market conditions, estimate fluctuations in prices and find the most profitable lines of export (or import-substitution) activities, subject to the supply constraints. On the sectoral level, it is again in Hungary that long-term programmes have been developed for several sectors. A simple type of model has been used for the cotton industry.[1] It uses as constraints the output figures (for domestic consumption and for exports) fixed by the plan for the last year of the long-term plan period, and attempts to expand the capacity of the sector so as to comply with these targets (mainly by investment changes). The objective function prescribes the minimization of all the discounted costs incurred during the period. Foreign trade enters into this type of problem only indirectly.

However, it plays a more important role in the plans worked out for the synthetic fibre branch, where only the domestic requirements for the products in period $t+n$ are given as a constraint determined by the plan, and output targets are a variable.[2] The problem becomes that of determining the best way of satisfying the given demand, i.e. that of finding an optimum mix between internal production and foreign trade. Thus a choice must be made, for instance, between producing many types of goods and producing just a few on a mass scale and exploiting the possibility of large-scale economies. In such a case the cost function would cease to be linear. The objective function used does in fact involve the minimization of costs needed to satisfy the domestic requirements for synthetic fibres, under the special assumption that income from possible exports reduces total costs. Mathematically the problem consists in minimizing a concave function subject to linear constraints (i.e. a form not of linear but of quadratic programming). A further, similar model was worked out for the aluminium

[1] Kornai, 'Mathematical Programming', p. 3.
[2] Ibid. pp. 3–4.

industry.[1] It also attempted to minimize future costs and, at the same time, optimize foreign trade, by considering imports as positive and exports as negative costs and by taking into account all the direct and indirect foreign trade needs for given increments in production, investment, wage costs and material costs. This was done by a much more detailed study of input–output relations, which were thus incorporated into the general linear programming model.

However, none of these models claims to be a substitute for traditional methods. While the short-term foreign trade optimization programmes can lead to a better export or import structure than present planning techniques allow, the longer-term mathematical formulations, at present at least, can only 'recommend changes with respect to the original trend of activities',[2] and thus achieve some saving of resources. As Kornai says, 'it would be idle speculation at present to dwell on the extent to which mathematical models will, in the more distant future, be able to replace the traditional methods',[3] even though it is in Hungary that the greatest advances are apparently being made in the field of prospective mathematical planning.[4] Though Kornai's pessimism is probably appropriate as far as long-term plans are concerned, it is less so for the short-term models. Despite Soviet scepticism,[5] it can no longer be said that all the programming techniques so far elaborated have been merely interesting but inapplicable mathematical exercises. Experiments have been increasing in the three countries where the study of programming techniques is most advanced. Some models have been applied in Poland (in the vegetable oils[6] and shipbuilding industries[7]) and in East Germany several sectors have been studied (e.g. chemicals, wood and paper[8]).

---

[1] J. Kornai and B. Martos, 'The Application of the Input-Output Table to determine the optimum Development Program of the Aluminium Industry', in O. Lukacs (ed.), *Input-Output Tables*.

[2] Kornai, 'Mathematical Programming...', p. 5.   [3] Ibid. p. 1.

[4] Kornai, 'Mathematical Programming as a tool in drawing up the Five-Year Economic Plan', *Economics of Planning*, Vol. v, No. 3, 1965.

[5] G. Shagalov, 'Ekonomicheskaya effektivnost vneshnyei torgovli sotsialisticheskich stran', *Voprosy Ekonomiki*, No. 6, June 1965, p. 99.

[6] Trzeciakowski, 'Model tekuschchei optimisatsyi', pp. 27–8.

[7] Grote, 'Zur Anwendung matematischer Methoden', p. 11.

[8] G. Appenfelder and P. Sydow, 'Zu praktischen Problemen bei der Optimierung der Regionalstruktur gegenüber kapitalistischen Ländern', *Der Aussenhandel*, No. 5, May 1964, p. 20.

In one, a textile machinery division, some of the indications given by the model were included in the 1965 foreign trade plan and were apparently used again in 1966.[1]

The way seems open for an increasing use of these techniques, since their results usually show an improvement (in foreign currency revenue) over and above the current plans worked out by the more traditional methods. It is true that the scope for improvement is not as large as may seem to be the case if one considers only the inadequacy of the traditional methods since, for most of the Eastern European countries, by far the largest part of foreign trade is already fixed in terms of long-run bilateral contracts with other socialist countries and, therefore, usually given as a constraint.[2] In the Hungarian case, for instance, linear programming techniques can be applied to only 20 per cent of total foreign trade turnover.[3] Further limitations arise from the linearity assumptions—constant costs, whenever domestic costs are taken into account, and constant foreign prices, not influenced by the foreign trade actions of the country. The latter assumption, however, may not be too heroic in the case of the smaller Eastern European countries, whose weight in the foreign markets for most commodities is unlikely to be large.[4] Where it could be, i.e. in the case of a few of the Soviet Union's imports and exports, non-linearity of world prices is assumed in a very general model, not primarily concerned with foreign trade, developed by Konius.[5]

A more important criticism aimed at linear programming methods is voiced by a United Nations survey (drawing mainly on the Polish experience) which points out that 'there are no inherent connections between the systems of effectiveness analysis, premia and accounting',[6] thus: 'in practice, the discretionary powers left to management in the process of plan implementation are quite considerable, particularly in

[1] von Krepl and Gollmer, 'Erfahrungen des A.H.U. Invest Export', p. 12.
[2] A. Zauberman, *Aspects of Planometrics*, London 1967, p. 212.
[3] Marton and Tardos, 'Short-run Optimization', p. 77.
[4] In any case, the relative stability of prices in intra-CMEA transactions lessens the short-run impact of any fluctuations in world prices.
[5] A. A. Konius, 'Raschirenie sistemi uravnenyi mezhotraslovich sviasei dlya tselei perspektivnogo planirovanya', in V. S. Nemchinov (ed.), *Primenenie matematiki v ekonomicheskich isledovanyach*, Moscow 1961, Vol II, pp. 71–2
[6] United Nations, Economic Commission for Europe, *Economic Survey 1962*, Part II, Ch. 4, p. 52.

enterprises producing for export, [so that] there is obviously a contradiction between existing criteria of successful management and the criteria of foreign trade optimization'.[1] Hence, what is needed for a more rational foreign trade structure is needed whether the scope of reforms is to be limited to a more efficient use of the traditional indicators or optimization techniques are adopted, namely: 'A complete revision of the premium and financial system of enterprises in close contact with foreign trade, a far-reaching revision of the price system or, most probably, a combination of both approaches.'[2]

[1] Ibid p. 54.   [2] Ibid.

7

MACRO-ECONOMIC CRITERIA
AND GROWTH STRATEGY

The preceding discussion has, more often than not, been conducted in relatively static terms. It has also been oriented mainly towards the achievement of some sort of micro-economic rationality, that would allow correct choices between tradeable commodities in the presence of domestic distortions. But probably the main characteristic of Soviet-type economies, at least until now, has been their stress on dynamic factors and on very broad macro-economic choices between large sectors. 'Balanced growth' has been a concept alien to Eastern European practice, if not theory,[1] and the economic history of the Soviet Union and of the smaller Eastern European countries is strewn with choices between various priority sectors and concerted drives to achieve them. The origin of such a strategy goes back, on the one hand, to Marx's preference for industry over agriculture as the more developed and progressive form of economic organization, and on the other, to the underdeveloped condition of Russia in 1917, when the Bolshevik party took power. The contrast between the desired industrial state and the actual backward and overwhelmingly agrarian society in which power had been acquired was glaring. The solution to this contrast was to be found in a concerted, all-out strategy that was to give absolute priority to industry over agriculture and to department I goods (producers' goods), as against department II goods (consumer goods), within the industrial sector.[2]

Fine micro-economic choices were, of course, lost in such a policy and so too, regrettably, was the role of foreign trade.

---

[1] N. Spulber, *Soviet Strategy for Economic Growth*, Bloomington, Indiana 1964, Ch. 3.

[2] The debate over industrialization was, in fact, very sophisticated and none of its main proponents probably envisaged the actual form which forced industrialization (and forced collectivization) were to take in the First Five Year Plan. But all currents of opinion, Left, Right and Centre, as they were then defined, were in favour of rapid industrialization: A. Erlich, *The Soviet Industrialization Debate, 1924–1928*, Cambridge, Mass. 1960.

The abundant literature on growth strategy that flourished in the 1920s in the Soviet Union and that developed, or hinted at, so many concepts since 'discovered' by the present-day theory of economic development, was singularly reticent on foreign trade.[1] In the case of Russia, this relative silence can be explained both by the small role played by international trade in the economy and by the isolation of the country, reinforced by fears of imminent aggression from the West. It might have been hoped that in the smaller Eastern European countries the literature on how to plan foreign trade within a strategy based on priority sectors would have been more abundant, given the importance of trade to the countries concerned and the existence of a socialist world market. But the atmosphere of the early 1950s, when such macro-economic choices were being made, was hardly conducive to serious intellectual research of any kind. A Soviet, or better, Stalinist, development pattern was forced upon Eastern Europe and the role of foreign trade was neglected.

It is not easy, therefore, to define the macro-economic criteria that have dictated Eastern European foreign trade policy. Broad, normative statements have been made from time to time, but they are often contradictory. Generally it has been thought advisable to export capital-intensive products and to purchase labour-intensive ones abroad. Thus, for instance, it is held that Hungary's foreign trade and production enjoy a more 'favourable ratio' than Austria's, because Austria's exports of machinery are relatively much lower than Hungary's and, furthermore, Austria suffers from a deficit in machinery trade.[2] But on developmental grounds exactly the opposite policy has also been defended. Thus it has been argued in the DDR that imports of machinery should be preferred, since they represent a 'growth factor', while imports of raw materials are only a 'material precondition for growth'.[3] In Hungary, on the other

---

[1] Only a few references to foreign trade appear in Preobrazhensky's *The New Economics*, and almost none in a long collection of Soviet articles devoted to growth problems: N. Spulber (ed.), *Foundations of Soviet Strategy for Economic Growth: Selected Soviet Essays, 1924–1930*, Bloomington, Indiana 1964.

[2] I. Vajda, *The Role of Foreign Trade in a Socialist Economy*, Budapest 1965, pp. 90–2.

[3] G. Kohlmey, 'Karl Marx' Aussenhandelstheorie und Probleme der aussenwirtschaftlichen Beziehungen zwischen sozialistischen Staaten', *Wirtschaftswissenschaft*, No. 8, August 1967, p. 1242.

hand, because of raw material scarcity, it is the raw materials that become a 'growth factor', though the planners have recently attempted to minimize the development of branches with a high content of imported raw materials.[1]

An earlier East German statement, which would seem to contradict the arguments above, favours labour-intensive exports (presumably manufactures) as opposed to raw-material-intensive ones.[2] But to a Bulgarian economist, arguing with an eye to the problems of developing countries, labour-intensive methods of production are anathema even if they ensure full employment, since the country adopting them will lag behind partner countries in terms of technological development.[3] The encouragement of exports of manufactures rather than of raw materials has been defended more reasonably by a Polish economist, on the grounds that manufacturing production furthers all-round economic development and lessens dependence on world markets.[4] Another broad principle, inherited from the 1920s, has been the bias against imports of consumer goods. The theory behind this attitude was developed by Preobrazhensky and has since fitted well with the general strategy of the Eastern European economies.[5] Its corollary should, of course, be the encouragement of consumer goods exports but, apart from agricultural products, this strategy has not really been followed, since it would contradict the more basic aim of developing machinery exports.[6]

Autarky versus foreign trade

In this maze of confusing and contradictory statements, some broad policy lines can, however, be traced. The first is a general tendency towards autarky, the second the use of

---

[1] I. Vajda, *Foreign Trade in a Socialist Economy*, p. 135.

[2] R. Brauer, 'Zur Frage des volkswirtschaftlichen Nutzeffekts des Aussenhandels', *Wirtschaftswissenschaft*, No. 3, March 1958.

[3] K. Zarev, 'Mezhdunarodnaya spetsialisatsiya proisvodstva i kompleksnoe rasvitie ekonomiki otdelnich sotsialisticheskich stran', *Planovoe Khozyaistvo*, No. 4, April 1964, p. 29.

[4] M. Rakowski, *Efficiency of Investment in a Socialist Economy*, Oxford 1966, pp. 276–7.

[5] E. Preobrazhensky, *La Nouvelle Economique* (translated from the Russian by B. Joly), Paris 1966, pp. 156–62.

[6] It would also require a much larger volume of investment in the consumer goods sector. Even if only for exports, such an investment strategy runs counter to all the beliefs of Eastern European planners.

foreign trade to support the growth strategy. Autarky was pursued quite consciously both in the late 1930s in the Soviet Union and in the early 1950s in the other Eastern European countries. The traumatic experience of young Soviet Russia threatened from all corners, and the profoundly insular and nationalistic mentality of Stalin, combined in dictating a foreign trade strategy that was in fact no strategy at all, but just an attempt to cut links with the rest of the world.[1] Admittedly autarky was never complete, it was often disclaimed as an official aim,[2] and even when it was proclaimed, it was unsuccessful,[3] but it remains true that foreign trade potentials were not really exploited to their full advantage by the Eastern European countries for a long time.[4] Only since the middle of the 1950s has autarky been rejected, at first tacitly and later openly, and the dangers of excessive under-specialization understood. The volume of foreign trade that remained, however, fulfilled a definite function—that of earning foreign exchange, which was in its turn considered as 'essentially an investment resource'.[5] Thus foreign trade became one of the elements contributing to the growth-maximizing policy of the Eastern European countries. As an *ex post* rationalization, some of the interactions between the limited volume of foreign trade undertaken and the growth process experienced in Eastern Europe are tentatively sketched below.[6]

---

[1] This is not quite true of the First Five Year Plan, during which trade with the West was conducted on quite a large scale, despite the disastrous fall in Russia's export prices. It is strange, in fact, how little part the terms of trade played in the early days of Eastern European planning. A very large volume of foreign trade was carried on by the Soviet Union just when the terms of trade turned sharply against her. And in the very early 1950s, when primary product prices skyrocketed under the influence of the Korean War, the smaller Eastern European countries whose comparative advantage lay, with the exception of East Germany and Czechoslovakia, in agriculture and raw material production, embarked on an all-out drive for industrialization, turning their backs on the opportunities offered by foreign trade.

[2] G. Rubinshtein, 'Rasvitie Sovetskogo importa', *Vneshnyaya Torgovlya*, No. 5, May 1960, p. 3.

[3] Wiles, *Communist International Economics*, pp. 437–44.

[4] F. L. Pryor, *Communist Foreign Trade System*, London 1963, pp. 23–8.

[5] Wiles, *Communist International Economics*, p. 187.

[6] A short model for Soviet foreign trade which, though not identical to the one developed here, has some similarities, is sketched by F. D. Holzman in 'Foreign Trade', in A. Bergson and S. Kuznets (eds.), *Economic Trends in the Soviet Union*, Cambridge, Mass., 1963.

In the static two-country, two-factor, two-good model of international trade theory, it cannot be denied that autarky leads to a sub-optimal consumption structure, while foreign trade maximizes present satisfactions. Such a simple model can, nevertheless, be used, at least as a starting point, to give some indication of the role of foreign trade in a centrally planned

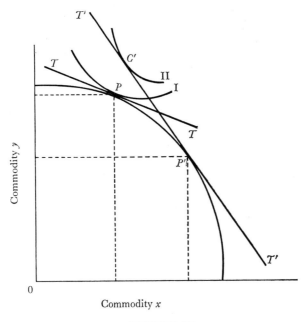

FIGURE 10

economy. Figure 10 shows the various possible outputs of two commodities which can be defined as an investment good y, and a consumption good x (epitomized, for brevity, as 'machinery' and 'wheat' respectively). The relative amounts produced of these two commodities will depend on the planners' preferences as expressed by the indifference curve I (of which, however, only one or, at most, few points have any operational significance), and by the domestic price line TT. The latter will be seen to reflect the relatively high valuation put by the central planning authority on investment goods, in comparison with the relative price line $T'T'$, pertaining to the rest of the world. Given these assumptions, the autarkic economy will both produce and consume at point P, while a similar economy, if it were to engage in foreign trade, could reach the higher community indifference curve II, by specializing in the production of good x and trading along the world price line, thus producing at P' and consuming at C'.[1]

Before continuing, some of the very theoretical abstractions may be considered. First, the assumption that points on the outer edge of the production possibility surface can be reached is very dubious. In market economies the existence of unemployment, monopolistic and oligopolistic distortions, etc., make such an event extremely unlikely. Similarly in centrally planned economies an artificial price structure prevents the optimal use of resources. The use of production points lying within the boundary and implying, therefore, some unemployment of resources, is probably more realistic and does not invalidate any of the arguments that follow.[2] Secondly, the use of community indifference curves has often been criticized, since their construction, in market economies, depends on the possibility of compensations or 'neutral' money transfers.[3] In the case of the planned economies, however, as already mentioned,[4] their use is more justified, as a 'real' set of planners' preferences has much more of an existence than the fictitious community indifference curves set up for market economies.

Returning to the example sketched above, it would appear that the market economy is faring much better than the planned one. It can be argued, however, that the model reflects reality only at a given moment of time and takes into account neither the dynamic effects which different production structures may have on future developments nor, of course, the different political courses which the two countries may have

---

[1] It is assumed that this alternative economy is a competitive free trade one, while the intermediate case of a planned economy taking full advantage of the possibilities of foreign trade (the Lange–Lerner type of economy examined in Chapter 2) is not considered here, since it has not, until very recently, been a practical possibility.

[2] The assumption could, in any case, be maintained in a situation of comprehensive planning through shadow prices, which in a planned economy is equivalent to perfect competition in a market economy.

[3] T. Scitovsky, 'A Reconsideration of the Theory of Tariffs', in The American Economic Association, *Readings in the Theory of International Trade*, London 1950; M. Dobb, *Welfare Economics and the Economics of Socialism*, Cambridge 1969.

[4] See Chapter 2.

chosen. The autarkic strategy of the centrally planned economy may not seem as illogical as at first sight if the country has, for political reasons, decided to minimize dependence on unreliable foreign markets and to promote rapid industrialization. Not only will the planned economy have abolished all ties with foreign countries but, as will be seen from Figure 10, having chosen the autarkic course, it will be producing a much larger amount of machinery than the free trade country. It is true that the latter may consume a greater amount of both commodities (this will depend on the preferences of the consumers), while the former will be producing machinery at greater cost than on the world market, but it can be argued that the dynamic effects of a large output of domestically produced investment goods may well outweigh, in the next stage or stages, the advantages of having a larger quantity of machinery immediately available, through acquired skills, economies of scale, external economies, etc. As has been said, 'machines are a "growth product"', and have an 'educative' function.[1]

This argument is reinforced by the fact that, when both economies grow, the one practising free trade is likely to specialize further in the production of the consumption good, while the centrally planned economy may well willingly distort its original comparative advantage pattern away from the production of wheat to that of machinery. In a perfect world this could be considered uneconomical, unless a clear-cut case of an infant industry could be presented, when even neo-classical free-trade economists would accept some degree of State interference.[2] But in an imperfect and dynamic world, in which it is often argued that the terms of trade have been deteriorating against raw materials and primary products (and possibly against most semi-manufactures as well), and in which the greatest productivity gains are probably scored in industrial production, the latter course may well hold greater promise, if not for the present or immediate future, at least in the longer run. It is not argued here that autarky is better than free trade, but only that, given a consistent development

---

[1] P. J. D. Wiles, 'Foreign Trade of Eastern Europe: A Summary Appraisal', in A. A. Brown and E. Neuberger (eds.), *International Trade and Central Planning*, Berkeley and Los Angeles 1968, p. 170.

[2] G. Haberler, *International Trade and Economic Development*, Cairo 1959, pp. 34–5.

strategy, the former course, which implies the reinvestment of most currently produced capital goods in the capital goods industry (as was explicitly assumed in the early years of Soviet planning),[1] may stimulate growth more than a purely free trade development process in which, presumably, the capital goods obtained from abroad will be invested mainly in the primary sector.

The 'pure autarky' assumption can now be relaxed. As is well known, self-sufficiency was never total even under the most stringent of the Soviet Five Year Plans, and some foreign trade

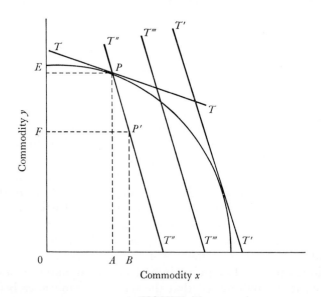

FIGURE II

was always carried on. Figure 11, therefore, introduces a moderate degree of international trade into the economy. Autarky is still defined as production and consumption at point P, but this point is also compatible with the moderate degree of specialization implied by trading along the terms of trade line $T''T''$ (parallel to $T'T'$), fixed by world market price

[1] E. D. Domar, 'A Soviet Model of Growth', in *Essays in the Theory of Economic Growth*, New York 1957; and review of E. Preobrazhensky's 'The New Economics', *Soviet Studies*, Vol. XVIII, No. 2, October 1966, p. 252.

relations. It can be assumed, for instance, that instead of producing a volume of consumption goods equal to $0A$, output is
pushed further and an amount $0B$ is produced. The increment
AB is then exchanged for an amount EF of capital goods along
the $T''T''$ line. The use of the latter price line and not of the
consumption-maximizing one $T'T'$ implies that, with respect
to consumption, the country is exactly as well off as before.
This, of course, is in line with the growth-maximising policy
objectives of the planners who, helped admittedly by the
political and administrative powers at the disposal of the
government, are able to fix the absolute amount of consumer
goods allowed to the population, by themselves determining
the accumulation rate of the economy. In such a case, which
corresponds broadly to the reality of Soviet and Eastern
European practice, the function of foreign trade is not, as in a
market economy, that of maximizing consumers' satisfaction
but that of promoting economic growth.

In Figure 11 the consequence of introducing some foreign
trade is a shift in the use of machinery away from some domestic
products to foreign ones (plus a shift in production from P to
P'). If the investment good is homogeneous and the centrally
planned economy produces the commodity in question as
efficiently as the rest of the world, the only apparent effect of
foreign trade would be some unemployment of resources, since
the outer bound of the production possibilities curve is not
reached. In a market economy this would hardly be described
as a desired result but, according to most Eastern European
economists, it is precisely this apparent unemployment which
is the most important benefit that can be obtained through
foreign trade, since it implies a saving in resources.[1] In
economies in which the supply of factors of production is the

---

[1] A long list of authors can be found, stressing this very classical point: e.g.
for Czechoslovakia: V. Cerniansky, 'Problems of the Economic Efficiency of
Foreign Trade', *Czechoslovak Economic Papers*, No. 1, Prague 1959; for Poland:
W. Trzeciakowski, 'Model tekuschchei optimisatsyi vneshnyei torgovli i ee
primenenie', *Vneshnyaya Torgovlya*, No. 6, June 1964, p. 20; for East Germany:
C. Hecht, 'Methoden und Kennziffern zur Ermittlung des Nutzeffektes der
sozialistischen internationale Arbeitsteilung', *Der Aussenhandel*, Part 1, No. 7, July
1964, p. 24; for the Soviet Union: A. Borisenko, 'K voprosu ob effektivnosti
sotsialisticheskoi vneshnyei torgovli', *Vneshnyaya Torgovlya*, No. 10, October 1964,
p. 9; for Bulgaria: E. G. Mateev, *Mezhdunarodnoe sotsialisticheskoe rasdelenie truda
i narodnokhozyaistvennoe planirovanye*, Moscow 1965, p. 29.

main limitation on growth[1] and in which the use of resources is usually strained to the limit,[2] any sparing of productive factors through foreign trade is welcome in so far as it permits a reallocation towards the investment sector of, say, capital and labour.

This saving can be shown in terms of an Edgeworth box diagram, as in Figure 12, in which the pre-trade production

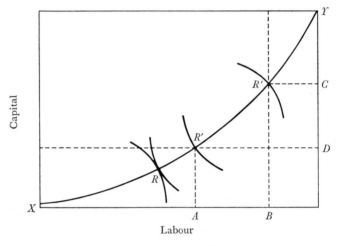

FIGURE 12

point (corresponding to point P in Figures 10 and 11) is shown as point R on the 'contract curve'. At point R all the available factors of production are fully used. With the introduction of foreign trade, production will be shifted from point R to the two points R' (corresponding to point P' in Figure 11), at which some more factors will be used for the production of good x (the

[1] W. Brus and K. Laski, 'Problems of the Theory of Growth under Socialism' in E. A. G. Robinson (ed.), *Problems in Economic Development*, London 1965, p. 23.
[2] More recently, however, the existence of some unemployment has been admitted in the Soviet Union: E. Manevich, 'Vseobshchnost truda i problemy ratsionalnogo ispolzovanyia rabochei sily v S.S.R.', *Voprosy Ekonomiki*, No. 6, June 1965. Further, the existence of labour migration within CMEA from Rumania and Bulgaria to East Germany and Czechoslovakia (J. Morgan, 'Rumania stands firm', *New Statesman*, Vol. LXX, No. 1793, 23 July 1965) implies some degree of underemployment or disguised unemployment in the less-developed members of the area.

consumer good), fewer for the production of good y (the producers' good) *and* some will be left unemployed. This availability of factors of production will be equal to amounts AB of labour and CB of capital. Thus, through foreign trade, a further 'surplus' of resources has been obtained, which can supplement the surplus already made available through the restriction of consumption. In the next planning period,[1] these saved resources can be used in the production of investment goods. As factors are reallocated, a larger production of machinery will be made possible and the production possibility curve itself will probably shift in a north-easterly direction as economies of scale are achieved and as the supply of labour increases. Some foreign trade will still be carried on, since the argument so far outlined still applies. It is, of course, also possible that the country may become self-sufficient and that a 'dialectical way to autarky' may be found, by trading at first and then retreating into self-sufficiency. But this course, which could only have been feasible, within limits, in the Soviet Union, has definitely been rejected in all the centrally planned economies.

So far only the 'saving in resources' theme has been developed. But, of course, the contribution of foreign trade to the growth of a centrally planned economy goes beyond this, if the assumption of one homogeneous type of 'machinery' equally produceable at home and abroad, is relaxed. If, in fact, the semi-autarkic economy can obtain a different or better product from abroad, then, apart from the possible saving in labour and capital, two added benefits can be reaped: the first directly linked to the larger output possible as a result of importing the superior machine, the second of a more indirect, 'learning' character, allowing in future planning periods the copying of the advanced foreign design and its reproduction at home.[2] A further assumption can now be relaxed, since it is both

---

[1] For purposes of exposition, the analysis is divided into successive planning periods, but it is of course possible that the resources saved through foreign trade are reinvested within the same planning period in so far as their availability is already approximately known, given a perspective foreign trade plan and some assumptions about the terms of trade.

[2] The latter seems to have occurred in the Soviet Union in the 1930s, when even single examples of Western machinery were imported and then copied, following a Japanese precedent already set in the nineteenth century: W. W. Lockwood, *The Economic Development of Japan*, Princeton 1954, pp. 320–46; A. Maddison, *Economic Growth in Japan and the USSR*, London 1969, p. 103.

plausible and likely that the centrally planned economy, instead of trading along the price line $T''T''$ (of Figure 11) will, at least beyond a certain stage of development, trade along the price line $T'''T'''$ instead. Such a move will be dictated not only by economic motives, but also by such intangible reasons as diminished fears of 'capitalist encirclement', the possibility of trade with other socialist countries, or the decreased danger of excessive specialization, once some progress towards industrialization has been made.[1] In fact, trade can be carried on along any of the parallels between the pure autarky and the free trade price lines; the one chosen will depend mainly on the degree of autarky preferred by the economy. Initially, the arguments so far developed will be valid; all the resources saved as a result of foreign trade will be reinvested, consumption will be fixed at an amount $0A$ and the 'income–consumption' curve will develop along the line PC, as shown in Figure 13, with relative prices (and wages) being such as to allow only the amount of consumption fixed beforehand for the population. Later, however, once the greater investment effort has been accomplished and a certain degree of industrialization achieved, some relaxation is likely *vis-à-vis* the consumer, and the curve showing points of contact between the production possibility curves and the consumption mixes decided upon by the planners could, for example, develop along the line CC' of Figure 13.

So far the influence of foreign trade on growth has been relatively marginal. It is an auxiliary to an 'extensive' growth process which is mainly furthered by a rising proportion of

[1] The existence of a CMEA market has made the process sketched above much less painful for some of the developing Eastern European countries than it was for the Soviet Union. The latter was faced by a hostile world and by falling export prices. The former, after the initial period of post-war adjustment and reparation payments, were able to further their industrialization with the help of credits from Russia, the DDR and Czechoslovakia, and could count on stable terms of trade and on a ready demand for their products. While aid *strictu sensu* may not have been very important, the two other factors appear to have been much more significant. It is thus through 'trade, not aid' that China and Albania, until the Sino-Soviet rift, and Bulgaria until now, have benefited from a Socialist world market; W. Galeson, 'Economic Relations between the Soviet Union and Communist China' in N. Spulber (ed.), *Study of the Soviet Economy*, Bloomington, Indiana 1961, pp. 34–8; M. Kaser, *Comecon* (2nd edition), London 1967, pp. 105–6; J. M. Montias, *Economic Development in Communist Rumania*, Cambridge, Mass. 1967, p. 235; P. J. D. Wiles, 'Foreign Trade of Eastern Europe', pp. 399–405.

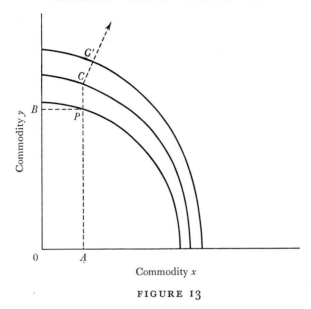

FIGURE 13

investment in national income and is, therefore, similar to a
simple Harrod–Domar growth model, in which the savings
rate and the capital–output ratio, at a constant rate of population growth, play the most important role, while the function of
technical progress is neglected.[1] (The trade balance would not
enter into a centrally planned economy's growth function,
since trade is usually balanced with each country.) At present,
however, the advantages which can be obtained by greater
specialization, i.e. by trading further and further along terms
of trade lines to the right of $T''T''$, though still to the left of
$T'T'$ (as shown in Figure 11), are more frequently accepted in
Eastern European literature. In terms of the model so far used
this development implies a greater degree of specialization in
the production of the consumer good. This is a likely but not a
necessary outcome, since it ignores the possibility that the
country may, in the process, have changed its comparative
advantage pattern. Should it have done so, the previous
growth process would have created an already industrialized

[1] C. P. Kindleberger, *Foreign Trade and the National Economy*, New Haven 1962,
    pp. 191–4.

society which would now be able to export some types of machinery in exchange for others (assuming that more than one capital good exists), or even to exchange its producers' goods for imported primary products. In fact, the former type of exchange is the most likely and examples of it can be found as early as the 1930s in the Soviet Union.[1] It seems now to be quite common in the USSR[2] and in other Eastern European countries, as witnessed by the increasing share of machinery in the total exports of, for instance, Poland, Rumania and Bulgaria.[3]

The role of foreign trade in the planned economies

The influence of foreign trade on the growth process of centrally planned economies, as sketched above, evidently differs from that usually associated with the experience of market economies, either developed or underdeveloped. In the case of Western industrialized economies, the influence of foreign trade operates mainly through exports. This can happen either in a Keynesian underemployed type of world, in which export demand, through the foreign trade multiplier, supplements an insufficient domestic effective demand, or in a post-war full-employment society, in which growth can often be 'export-propelled',[4] by virtue of a spiral of investment-stimulating increases in productivity, which in their turn promote exports; thanks to the latter, balance of payments constraints can be ignored and further high investment plans launched, which keep the economy in a state of long-run confidence, itself generator of further and faster growth.

In underdeveloped countries, by contrast, the growth factor comes from imports.[5] The latter provide the required tech-

[1] J. P. Saltiel, 'Commerce extérieur et industrialisation—L'expérience des années 1930–1931', *Cahiers de l'I.S.E.A.*, Série G (No. 13), No. 124, April 1962, p. 128.
[2] G. Adler-Karlsson, 'The Semi-developed Soviet Economy—A Foreign Trade Illustration', *Economics of Planning*, Vol. VI, No. 1, 1966.
[3] J. M. Montias, 'Socialist Industrialization and Trade in Machinery Products', in Brown and Neuberger (eds.), *International Trade*.
[4] W. Beckerman, 'Projecting Europe's Growth', *The Economic Journal*, Vol. LXXII, No. 288, December 1962.
[5] Theoretically, this is of course true for all economies, as the application of a Harrod–Domar growth model to an open economy can show. In such a model the growth rate of the economy is positively related to the inverse of the marginal

niques and capital goods which the economy is incapable of producing itself. In such cases a more appropriate tool would seem to be that of an 'import-multiplier', which would relate either absolute growth or increases in the rate of growth to the import of necessary capital goods. The case of the centrally planned economies is, in many ways, intermediate and it is for that reason that, if a label were to be attached to them, they could be defined as 'semi-developed'.[1] At first their economic structures and growth needs resembled more closely those of underdeveloped countries, though it must not be forgotten that almost all of them had probably reached, before their socialist revolution, a much higher degree of development than that of most underdeveloped societies today. Their main problem was, therefore, not so much that of acquiring a whole gamut of capital goods that could not be produced at home as that of obtaining the maximum possible output, in terms of capital goods, from given resources, which had already achieved a degree of skill and sophistication sufficient to produce them.[2] Obtaining the maximum possible output is a necessity for underdeveloped countries as well, but it cannot be disputed that, because of extreme backwardness and/or the number of bottlenecks, this process was, and is, much more difficult and cannot be carried out without foreign trade and aid. For the centrally planned economies it was easier to limit the function of foreign trade to that of accessory to a development process fostered within a general autarkic frame.[3]

Reliance on certain macro-criteria for domestic growth, aided by a strictly controlled pattern of foreign exchanges, has allowed the Eastern European countries to industrialize rapidly, to avoid excessive specialization in one, or a few, primary

capital–output ratio and to the propensities to save *and* import, and negatively to the ratio of exports to income: H. G. Johnson, *International Trade and Economic Growth*, London 1958, Ch. 5; J. Soldaczuk, 'Foreign Trade and Economic Growth in the Socialist Economy', in J. Soldaczuk (ed.), *International Trade and Development: Theory and Policy*, Warsaw 1966.

[1] This definition is used by Adler-Karlsson, 'The Semi-developed Soviet Economy'; of course such a term masks the very important differences existing, for instance, between Czechoslovakia and East Germany on the one hand, and Bulgaria and Rumania (let alone Albania) on the other, and should, therefore, be considered as a very broad term of reference only partly reflecting reality.

[2] Erlich, *Soviet Industrialization Debate*, pp. 161–2.

[3] Partly because of the political conditions of the time, this development strategy seems also to have been the only one possible.

commodities and, probably, to alter the comparative advantage pattern which would have been dictated to them, at the outset, by strictly static considerations. In purely economic terms the strategy can be considered as having been successful. But it is precisely its success that makes the continuation of such a strategy almost impossible. Most of the old priority goals (electricity, steel, armaments) have by now been achieved. The range of possible choices has widened considerably (chemicals, consumer goods, increased leisure, electronics, agriculture, etc.). At the same time the supply of labour has become much less elastic as the earlier massive drift away from the countryside has turned into a trickle. The growth process is turning from an extensive into an intensive one. Possibilities are limited for further increases in output by mere plant multiplication. Marginal capital–output ratios are increasing, and very rapidly at times. The much more refined and difficult choices associated with capital deepening are taking the place of the rough-and-ready methods that for a long time had been directing capital into a few chosen sectors.

Foreign trade at such a stage has a more positive role to play. Instead of merely saving resources, the marginal product of which sharply declines in import-competing industries, it fulfils the more classical function of widening choices, creating economies of scale and, especially, stimulating technical progress. This latter function is achieved if the need to keep up with required international standards leads to a concentration of effort in export sectors.[1] Governments have come to recognize that import needs are potentially very large (rather than, as previously, seeking to suppress them), although they still regard exports as a regrettable necessity; consequently growth cannot be seen as export led, but dependence on foreign trade is increasing, and planned specialization, both inter- and intra-industrial, is being pursued. In these conditions imports perform a function similar to the one so far considered, but exports too begin to contribute (notwithstanding the attitude that they represent a 'loss' of domestic output), by encouraging the

[1] G. Kohlmey, 'Wirtschaftswachstum und Aussenhandel', *Der Aussenhandel*, No. 5, March 1965; and 'From Extensive to Intensive Economic Growth', *Czechoslovak Economic Papers*, No. 6, Prague 1966; V. Nachtigal, 'Extensity and Efficiency of Economic Growth in Czechoslovakia', *Czechoslovak Economic Papers*, No. 9, Prague 1967.

growth of leading sectors capable of stimulating the rest of the economy, and by helping to dismantle an 'under-specialized' economy in which a large number of commodities was produced in almost invariably inefficient conditions.

It is ironical that the stress laid on heavy industry is now creating foreign trade problems for several of the Eastern European countries. One of the main reasons for Czechoslovakia's difficulties in recent years has been its excessive stress on the production of too large a number of machines, in none of which investment and production scales were sufficient to make it really competitive. Difficulties have also been experienced by other Eastern European countries, notably Poland, which has been unable to sell its surplus equipment on the CMEA market in exchange for raw materials. Thus it is the primary producing countries of the area, notably the Soviet Union and Rumania, which are in a strong monopolistic position at present *vis-à-vis* other CMEA countries. And it is the existence of such exportable commodities which also allows Rumania to obtain superior Western products and, to some extent, lessen its ties with the other Eastern European countries. The more industrialized partners, on the other hand, often find themselves with unsaleable stocks of machinery and unsatisfied demands for primary products when total demands and supplies are balanced at CMEA level.[1]

This should not, however, be taken as an indictment of the growth pattern chosen. The broad strategy which lifted the Eastern European countries from underdevelopment to industrialization was probably correct. The relative neglect of primary products and the insufficient attention given to quality, which are at the root of the present inbalance between overproduction of machinery and scarcity of raw materials, could probably be corrected relatively quickly, and CMEA's efforts at specialization are clearly a step in this direction.[2] By

---

[1] Vajda, 'Problemen und Formen', pp. 227–8; J. Tauchman and J. Novozamsky, 'The Nature of the International Division of Labour under Socialism', *Czechoslovak Economic Papers*, No. 11, Prague 1969, p. 137.

[2] Though agriculture presents, admittedly, a more thorny problem. Even in this field, however, though practical reforms lag behind those adopted in the industrial sphere, a discussion quoted in Kaser's *Comecon* (pp. 210–11), shows that some authors in East Germany have gone as far as questioning the primacy of industry over agriculture.

rationalizing and concentrating industrial production and coordinating a material-balances type of planning at intra-community level, the CMEA commission is able to point both to probable scarcities in primary production and to excessive supplies of machinery. The old growth strategy is being abandoned by all the Eastern European countries, with the exception of Rumania; the functions which foreign trade is now expected to fulfil create an urgent need for the micro-economic rationality that has been discussed in previous chapters.

CONCLUSION

The foregoing analysis has given some indication of the growing importance which foreign trade is acquiring in the eyes of Eastern European planners. From the textbook cases of wheat versus machinery barters of the near-autarkic Soviet Union in the 1930s, the centrally planned economies have now reached the sophistication of linear programming models attempting to determine an optimal foreign trade structure under given institutional constraints. It seems fairly obvious that the broad lines of such a development were inevitable and that, beyond a certain point, a policy of complete autarky (had it ever been followed), could not have led, except for the briefest of time-spans, to the fast growth rates which were politically desired. Eastern European planners became conscious of this dilemma. At first they managed to achieve the planned growth rates in a context of qualified autarky (and even in this period the success of the autarky drives was only limited). Later on, autarky as a policy aim was more or less abandoned. Thus, as the Eastern European countries have approached a development stage like that already reached by the more advanced countries of Western Europe, the share of foreign trade in their national income has been growing. It can be argued that this share will increase further in the near future, as industrialization, intra-CMEA integration and diversification of growth proceed.

A rising share of foreign trade in national income is not necessarily a proof of the existence of a highly industrialized society or of a rapidly growing one. It has been argued, for instance, that for most of the Western developed countries this share has declined after a certain date, which has been put at before, or just after, World War I.[1] But even if this theory were true—and data for the 1960s, incorporating the effects of customs union creations, would probably (if only temporarily)

---

[1] K. W. Deutsch and A. Eckstein, 'National Industrialization and the Declining Share of the International Economic Sector, 1890–1959', *World Politics*, Vol. XIII, No. 2, January 1961; C. P. Kindleberger, *Foreign Trade and the National Economy*, New Haven 1962, pp. 177–94.

invalidate it—past experience would tend to show that the highest ratios of foreign trade to national income were attained in periods of very rapid, or already achieved, industrialization.[1] In the case of the centrally planned economies some such rapid industrialization had, of course, taken place in the early 1950s (and in the 1930s in the case of the Soviet Union), within an autarkic context. Thus some increase in foreign trade in later years was inevitable, but it would be difficult to deny that the recent growth of foreign trade in Eastern Europe has been above what would have resulted from a simple extrapolation of previous trends. It can only be ascribed to a conscious policy change dictated by the necessities of the growth process itself. Table 1 (p. 137) provides some indication of this. It shows estimated values of income elasticities of demand for imports (with respect to national income) for the Eastern European countries in the period 1950–68. The figures given in the table are subject to the serious reservation that the underlying statistical data very often vary in nature (and reliability), that definitions differ between countries, and that, in some cases, the figures have had to be derived from linked indices. Thus the table attempts to give only a very general impression of trends, while the orders of magnitude may well be misleading.

United Nations sources provide more or less consistent series in current prices for imports (customs figures) for the 1950–68 period for practically all countries. Data for Rumania were obtained from a recent study by Montias.[2] The trade figures there referred to as 'New Series' were used for the post-1955 years and an *ad hoc* interpolation had to be made for 1956 and 1957, with the help of the 'Old Series' data. Volume indicators would probably have been more suitable for this kind of analysis, as they would have excluded not only the effects of price changes intervening on the world and on the CMEA markets for imported commodities, but also those of sudden

---

[1] Thus, for instance, the highest share of foreign trade (average of exports and imports) in national income (or national income plus imports) up to 1960 was reached by the United Kingdom and Germany in the 1870–9 period, by Sweden in 1879–98, by the Netherlands in 1900–8, by France in 1920–8, by Japan in 1930–8 and by Italy in the post-war period; cf. Kindleberger, *Foreign Trade and the National Economy*, pp. 180–1.

[2] J. M. Montias, *Economic Development in Communist Rumania*, Cambridge, Mass. 1967, p. 137.

price reforms within each country. Unfortunately indices of
foreign trade unit values do not exist for all the countries concerned for a long enough period. The use of current values may
admittedly vitiate the results, but it is difficult to determine in
what direction and to what extent. The margin of error is in
any case limited by the practice of holding the prices of most
internationally traded goods at a fixed level for relatively long
periods. The value statistics thus approach constant price data,
and real distortions probably occur only at times of large price
reforms on the CMEA market.[1]

United Nations publications are also the main source for the
volume data on national income (net material product at
market prices as defined in Eastern Europe, i.e. excluding non-
productive services and including turnover taxes).[2] Some
unofficial sources were, however, used for the period 1950–5
for East Germany, the Soviet Union and Albania.[3] The income
elasticity of demand calculation is therefore based on a hybrid
of value and volume changes. While results based on volume
data only would have been preferable, the amount of distortion
introduced by using foreign trade data at semi-constant prices
ought not to be excessive. The results should still be sufficient

[1] G. J. Staller, 'Patterns of Stability in Foreign Trade: OECD and COMECON:
1950–1963', *The American Economic Review*, Vol. LVII, No. 4, September 1967,
p. 884.
[2] The use of this concept in Eastern European practice tends perhaps to over-
estimate the rate of growth of national income. In fact the share of agriculture
is usually undervalued because the agricultural sector's output is free from
turnover taxes and is frequently underpriced while, for the opposite reasons, the
share of industry is exaggerated. Given the latter's fast-increasing weight, a constant bias is fed into indicators of growth (though the amount of 'inflation' of
performance is limited by the relative undervaluation of capital-intensive
producers' goods, which are subject to neither interest rate nor turnover taxes
and whose production tended to grow, until recently at least, at a faster rate than
that of the rest of the industrial sector): cf. United Nations, Economic Commission for Europe, *Economic Bulletin for Europe*, Vol. XI, No. 3, November 1959,
pp. 52–68. The exclusion of *services*, on the other hand, would, *prima facie*, tend to
depress the growth rates of national income, since it is often argued that in
modern economies *services* is the fastest-growing sector. This, however, is not at all
certain. Data published by OECD show that for eight out of eleven developed
countries the share of services in GDP, at constant prices, declined between
1950 and 1965; OECD, *Economic Growth, 1960–1970*, Paris 1966, pp. 32–3.
The exclusion of such unproductive activities as advertising or public relations
would probably reinforce this trend, but in Eastern Europe this could be more
than compensated for by the faster growth of social services.
[3] See appendix for basic data and sources.

to serve as indicators of basic trends. Both national income and import figures are in terms of the national currencies of the countries concerned but, whenever available, import data expressed in 'foreign exchange' or *valuta* units were used. The latter are in fact equivalent to imports at foreign (or world) prices, and are, therefore, free from the distortions of the domestic price system. For some countries the price basis used in valuing imports is not known (though there is a strong presumption that all countries behave similarly and that foreign prices are used throughout). If domestic prices have been used, then the results obtained would probably not coincide with those that a series in foreign prices would have given, since imports valued at domestic prices differ from imports expressed in foreign prices. If the difference were to remain constant, no bias would be fed into the income elasticity of demand calculations, but if the amount of 'taxes' on imports (i.e. the difference between their cost abroad and their selling price at home) changes, as seems to have been the case at times, then the rate of growth of imports as calculated for the above table could be either under- or over-estimated.[1] Again it is difficult to reach any precise conclusion as to the direction or magnitude of this further possible error.

Given all these deficiencies, it must be reiterated that the figures in Table 1 should not be used as precise indicators, but only as an expression of very general trends. As such they tend to confirm the increasing role played by foreign trade in Eastern European growth over the period from 1950 to the middle of the 1960s. And though this development has been, almost uniformly, reversed in the latest period under observation, it is probable that this interruption will only be temporary. Broadly, the data for 1950–5 tend to confirm the 'relative autarky' hypothesis. The share of imports in national income seems to have declined in most countries in the group. Trade with the West was drastically cut, as a result of political pressures. Trade within the area grew rapidly, but the basically competitive (rather than complementary) structures of most Eastern European economies, combined with lack of co-ordination between them, limited trade opportunities. Two

---

[1] United Nations, Economic Commission for Europe, *Economic Survey of Europe in 1957*, Geneva 1958, Ch. 6, pp. 28–9.

TABLE I. *Income Elasticities of Demand for Imports^a in Eastern Europe, 1950–68*

	1950–5	1955–60	1960–4	1964–8
Bulgaria	0·96	2·17	2·19	1·60
Czechoslovakia	1·01	1·51	5·58	0·71
East Germany	(2·03)	1·59	1·71	1·25
Hungary	2·11	1·63	2·19	0·87
Poland	0·52	1·49	1·49	1·16
Rumania	0·81	0·83	1·78	1·25
Soviet Union	(1·42)	1·37	1·41	0·58
Albania	(0·60)	(2·64)	0·50	..

^{a} Percentage change in imports associated with a 1 per cent change in national income. Results are based on trend growth rates for each period in order to eliminate the influence of abnormal terminal years. Trend growth rates were obtained by fitting semi-logarithmic trend lines to the actual data. Lack of data prevented such calculations for figures shown in brackets which are based on average annual percentage changes.

SOURCES: See Appendix.

countries, however, stand out as glaring exceptions: East Germany and Hungary. In the case of East Germany the very high income elasticity for imports may well have been due to the necessity, cut off as the country was from its main source of supply (the other half of the country), to find alternative trade partners relatively fast (even in a period of enforced autarky), so as to avoid still further dislocation, and perhaps complete economic breakdown.[1] For Hungary the explanation is more complex, since it is precisely in that country over these years that 'the planners' opposition to the country's involvement in international division of labor was strongest'.[2] But the forced industrialization of a country like Hungary, almost entirely lacking a domestic raw material basis, was bound to increase, rather than decrease, import dependence. Most of the other

[1] The plausibility of this explanation seems to be confirmed, at least for the 1950–5 period, by the data for intra-German trade given in M. C. Kaser, *Comecon* (2nd edition), London 1967, p. 144; which show very low volumes of exchange in the years up to 1954. It is possible, therefore, that the East German economy was forced to rely more on (non-German) imports than other bloc countries.

[2] A. A. Brown, 'Towards a Theory of Centrally Planned Foreign Trade', in A. A. Brown and E. Neuberger (eds.), *International Trade*, Berkeley and Los Angeles 1968, p. 61.

Eastern European countries possessed some raw material endowment, so that the rapid growth of a steel sector, and of heavy industry generally, could to some extent be supported domestically. For Hungary this was not the case, and the stress laid on developing a self-sufficient industrial structure was bound to be self-defeating. The Soviet Union also experienced an income elasticity of demand for imports greater than unity, but in its case reparation payments from former enemies, notably East Germany,[1] and very favourable trade agreements with other Eastern European countries, for instance Hungary and Poland,[2] provide a partial explanation for the expansion of trade in this period.

Between 1955 and 1965 imports grew, almost uniformly, faster than national income. At first political liberalization at home, together with a lessening of international tensions, permitted a growth of foreign trade which domestic economic developments were making inevitable. And later on, trade was furthered by the activation of CMEA. Though the origins of the association date back to January 1949,[3] it was only gradually strengthened after 1956, when the first agreements providing for specialization of production in certain sectors were made.[4] Though these early agreements bore little fruit for some time,[5] by the end of the 1950s or early 1960s international co-operation was in full swing. Eastern European planners began to accept CMEA as a ready source of supply for commodities apart from badly needed Soviet raw materials or non-competitive Czech or East German machine tools. Table 2 shows the renewed importance of intra-CMEA trade for the centrally planned economies after about 1958–9, when it seems that specialization plans and long-term co-ordination began to be introduced.

Three countries show somewhat exceptional developments in this period: Bulgaria, Czechoslovakia and Rumania. In the case of Bulgaria, it is likely that the relatively large availability

---

[1] H. Köhler, *Economic Integration in the Soviet Bloc: with an East German Case Study*, New York 1965, pp. 328–31.
[2] United Nations, Economic Commission for Europe, *Economic Survey of Europe in 1957*, Geneva 1958, Ch. 6, p. 3.
[3] Kaser, *Comecon*, p. 225.
[4] Ibid. pp. 225–7.
[5] F. L. Pryor, *Communist Foreign Trade System*, London 1963, p. 47.

TABLE 2. *Share of intra-CMEA trade in total
CMEA exports*

	1938	1948	1958	1968	1950–4	1955–60	1960–4	1964–8
Total CMEA	..	..	58·7	60·1	61·1	59·5	63·2	60·8
CMEA excluding intra-German trade	1·0	44·3	59·9	60·9	61·8	60·6	64·2	61·7

SOURCES: See Appendix.

of credits from the Soviet Union, together with the very high
import content of the investment drive of the late 1950s, led
to a very sharp increase in import dependence,[1] which came
sooner than that of other partner countries and continued in the
early 1960s as a result of the all-out policy of integration into
CMEA which Bulgaria pursued.[2] As for Czechoslovakia, the
change in the value of the income elasticity between the two
periods is clearly too large to be a reflexion of reality. It is
probably linked to the great difficulties encountered by the
economy in recent years (the annual trend rate of growth of
national income in the period 1960–4 was barely 1·2 per cent),
but also, probably, to some statistical bias. Rumania's average
propensity to import, on the other hand, decreased further in
the later 1950s. It is true, however, that in relation to size and
economic development, Rumania was more dependent on
foreign trade than, for instance, Bulgaria in the early 1950s,
mainly because of its abundant exports of raw materials. As
industrialization was launched, the exportable surplus shrank,
and growth was mainly domestically propelled.[3] Involvement
in international trade came only later (and was therefore more

---

[1] In 1959 alone productive investment rose by 65 per cent and imports of
machinery and equipment by 73 per cent. The 1958–60 period has been called
that of the 'big leap' which has allowed an actual 'take off' in the country.
United Nations, Economic Commission for Europe, *Economic Survey of Europe
in 1957*, Ch. 6, pp. 36–7, and *Economic Bulletin for Europe*, Vol. XVIII, No. 1,
November 1966, pp. 31–5.
[2] United Nations, Economic Commission for Europe, *Economic Bulletin for Europe*,
Vol. XX, No. 2, March 1969, p. 34.
[3] Ibid. p. 32.

sudden),[1] as the output of primary products rose sufficiently to allow for a much greater volume of exports. As for the change in Albania's income elasticity of demand for imports, a ready answer can probably be found in the field of transport (or location) economics!

Several possible explanations spring to mind when looking at the figures in Table 1 for the 1964-8 period. Balance of payments difficulties, at one time or another, forced Hungary, Poland, Czechoslovakia, the DDR and Rumania to restrain the growth of imports. And the success of any individual country's restrictive policy could only lead partner countries into even greater difficulties. On average, agricultural production fared better during this period than in the immediately preceding years, thus lessening the need for food imports. Rumania was, at this time, not providing any support for cooperation within the area. And the introduction of a new price system in intra-CMEA trade probably altered the terms of trade in favour of manufactures and against raw materials.[2] Thus, for instance, the elasticities of demand of two raw-material-importing countries, Czechoslovakia and Hungary, are much lower in this period than those of the manufactures-importing countries, Bulgaria and Rumania. But East Germany does not fall so neatly into this pattern and, in any case, it can be argued on purely developmental grounds that such differences in elasticities would have existed anyway.

Probably the most important reason for the apparent slowdown was the lack of a precise pattern of exchanges and specialization laid down by CMEA and agreed upon by the member countries. The coming into operation of the 1966-70 plans led to a whole new set of agreements on specialization

[1] J. M. Montias, 'Unbalanced Growth in Rumania', *The American Economic Review*, Vol. LIII, No. 2 (Papers and Proceedings), May 1963, p. 569.

[2] The question of the introduction of a new price system is in a somewhat confused state. Prices were at first to be changed in January 1965. But the reform took longer than expected and was completed only in 1967, though all changes were, apparently, made retroactive to January 1966. While there does not seem to be any dispute on the question of how relative prices have moved, what has happened to the absolute price level is less clear. Thus the United Nation's Economic Commission for Europe predicted a reduction in the average price level in its 1965 Survey, but no change in the 1966 one; United Nations, Economic Commission for Europe, *Economic Survey of Europe in 1964*, Geneva 1965, Ch. 1, p. 49; *Economic Survey of Europe in 1965*, New York 1966, Part I, Ch. 1, p. 54; *Economic Survey of Europe in 1966*, New York 1967, Ch. 3, p. 2.

that had already been prepared in 1964, but which were not signed until 1966 or 1967. Thus 1966, for instance was a year of near stagnation in intra-CMEA trade (the share of exports going to partner countries fell from 64·1 per cent in 1964 to 59·1 per cent in 1966, the lowest level since 1958). By 1967, however, and even more by 1968, the growth of intra-imports had recovered quite sharply.[1] Thus it can be argued that the recent slowdown is only temporary and that the forces making for an increasing share of imports in the national income of the Eastern European countries will be at work again in the near future. This is confirmed by the information at present available on the 1966–70 plans, in which all the centrally planned economies plan for a faster growth of foreign trade than of total output.[2]

In this development CMEA is likely to play an increasing role. Of course, it cannot be considered as a classical case of a customs union, as defined by Viner or Meade,[3] even less as a free trade area. But it cannot be denied that some of the effects traditionally associated with a customs union can be ascribed to it. Thus international trade theory predicts that welfare gains can arise from the creation of a customs union, *inter alia*, through the achievement of economies of scale and forced changes in efficiency due to increased foreign competition, with further benefits obtainable through more dynamic, long-run, and intangible effects.[4] The advantages claimed for CMEA by a number of Eastern European economists go very much in the same direction and, though the 'foreign competition' effect cannot be of the same nature as in a market economy, it none the less exists, if a bilateral trade structure is

[1] United Nations, Economic Commission for Europe, *Economic Bulletin for Europe*, Vol. xix, No. 1, November 1967, p. 27; and Vol. xx, No. 1, November 1968, p. 21.
[2] United Nations, Economic Commission for Europe, *Economic Survey of Europe in 1966*, Ch. 3, p. 7; Z. J. Kamecki, 'The Problems of Foreign Trade Monopoly in a Socialist Economy', in J. Soldaczuk (ed.), *International Trade and Development—Theory and Policy*, Warsaw 1966, p. 18.
[3] J. Viner, *The Customs Union Issue*, New York 1950; J. E. Meade, *The Theory of Customs Unions*, Amsterdam 1955.
[4] R. G. Lipsey, 'The Theory of Customs Unions: A General Survey', in R. E. Caves and H. G. Johnson (eds.), *Readings in International Economics*, London 1968, p. 261; F. Gehrels and B. F. Johnston, 'The Economic Gains of European Integration', *The Journal of Political Economy*, Vol. lxiii, No. 4, August 1955, pp. 281–4.

replaced by a multilateral one in which possibilities of choice between various commodities of various qualities are allowed.[1] As for the traditional dilemma between trade diversion and trade creation, while the former is likely to have been very negligible in so far as much too much 'trade destruction' (and some trade diversion) had already taken place in the late 1940s and early 1950s, the trade creation effect has been, and probably still is, very important.[2] Of course, lower-cost suppliers are likely to exist outside CMEA for most traded commodities, but given the present political situation (and present cost structures), a wholesale switch towards such extra-CMEA sources is, as yet, unthinkable. It is probably true to say that for the East European countries trade within the bloc is not always the most desired form of exchange, and that supplies from Western European countries would be much preferred. However, given the great difficulties of earning freely convertible foreign currency and the political implications of altering radically the direction of the bulk of a country's trade (at present accepted, to a limited extent, only by Rumania), CMEA represents for them a 'second-best' form of customs union, in which some implicit protection against the rest of the world is granted to producers and in which growth of trade is stimulated not so much by falling tariff barriers and competition as by conscious planning. Indeed, it can be argued that the existence of this conscious planning is an advantage which CMEA has over a normal customs union and which provides CMEA with one of its stronger points. While specialization in a normal customs union follows the laws of the market and may well lead to the stagnation of some regions (witness the case of Southern Italy, after its unification with the North),[3] or the hypertrophy of others (as at present, in the Brussels–Essen–Strasbourg region of the EEC), the perspective plans of CMEA, and the policy of keeping foreign trade prices relatively constant, allow a much more rational pattern of specialization.

[1] G. L. Shagalov, *Ekonomicheskaya effektivnost tovarnogo obmena mezhdu sotsialisticheskimi stranami*, Moscow 1966, pp. 7–9.

[2] In this respect the general competitiveness of most CMEA members, already mentioned above, assures a large trade-creating effect, while the long-run specialization agreements, by making the economies complementary, reduce the dangers of trade diversion; Meade, *Theory of Customs Unions*, pp. 107–8.

[3] G. Luzzato, *L'economia italiana dal 1861 al 1894*, Torino 1968, pp. 23–8.

Rationality is, of course, here defined as a concern not for micro-economic efficiency and static comparative advantage, but for macro-economic dynamism and longer-run development problems.

It is true that the process of integration which has been pursued so far may not be fully carried out. It may be that some of the tendencies at present visible in Eastern Europe, added to the relaxation of political tension, will weaken intra-bloc ties in the near future so that the dynamic effects on trade and growth which can be associated with CMEA may tend to diminish.[1] However, until exchanges between East and West are more fully liberalized the centrally planned economies can finance only a limited volume of trade with the outside world (unless they obtain much larger and easier trade credits). The inability of the Eastern European countries substantially to increase their trade turnover with the West would seem to result mainly from their inflexible production structures.[2] The frequent changes in tastes which condition so many of the international trade flows of Western countries are probably unmanageable for Eastern European enterprises, which are used to cumbersome and detailed plans coming from above and unable to alter production mixes or techniques with any speed. The economic reforms will probably improve performance on this score, but it will be some time before most Eastern European enterprises will be able to compete successfully on world markets. In the meantime intra-CMEA trade has been growing faster than outside trade (the recent stagnation, as seen above, seems to be only temporary) and is likely to go on growing faster in the future, as many of the obstacles still hindering integration are slowly removed. The increasing degree of multi-lateralism and the not-too-remote possibility of convertibility[3]

[1] An important element in favouring increased exchanges with the West may be the apparent switch in planners' priorities towards consumption, notably in favour of durable consumers' goods, which has already led to a number of large contracts being signed with Western European firms.
[2] O. Sik, *Plan and Market under Socialism*, Prague 1967, p. 81; F. D. Holzman, 'Soviet Central Planning and Its Impact on Foreign Trade Behaviour and Adjustment Mechanisms', in A. A. Brown and E. Neuberger (eds.), *International Trade*, p. 299.
[3] The need for convertibility is more and more frequently being stressed in Eastern European literature: Sik, *Plan and Market under Socialism*, p. 330; G. Kohlmey, 'Karl Marx' Aussenhandelstheorie und Probleme der aussenwirt-

within the area are two as yet unexploited factors, which could act as powerful expansionary forces on intra-CMEA trade. The present plans for 1966–70 imply not only, as already mentioned, a faster increase in trade than in output, but also increases in intra-CMEA trade more rapid than those forecast for total trade.[1] And the scanty information available on the perspective plans for 1980 suggests a continuation of this development.[2]

The factors so far reviewed—the past experience of other industrialized countries, economic rationality, the present switch from extensive to intensive growth, administrative reforms, the development of CMEA—would all seem to point to a growing involvement in foreign trade. The dilemma of Eastern European planners is no longer that of choosing between a state of semi-autarky and trade. Once it has been accepted that the latter is an essential element in the growth process of all the Eastern European countries (except, possibly, the Soviet Union), any mistakes involved in its planning can have very serious consequences. A parallel might be the lack of refined interest rate calculations at a time when the major effort for growth was being conducted in the investment field. At that time waste was probably enormous, but at least the general economic strategy had been decided upon and, whatever the losses, advances were being made on a large front without too glaring inconsistencies. Nowadays economic waste on that scale is much less likely, but the number of variables between which choice has to be exercised has become much larger, and the need for precision much more vital. Misallocation of resources in the early days of central planning did not stop a gigantic growth process, but misallocation of resources at present can make the difference between growth and stagnation.

Hence the need for economic criteria in foreign trade, both

schaftlichen Beziehungen zwischen sozialistischen Staaten', *Wirtschaftswissenschaft*, No. 8, August 1967, p. 1252; and it is hoped that some degree of convertibility will be introduced in the 1970s in Hungary: B. Csikos-Nagy, *Pricing in Hungary*, London 1968, p. 33.
[1] B. Ladigin and Y. Shiraev, 'Voprosy sovershenstvovaniya ekonomicheskogo sotrudnichestva stran SEV', *Voprosy Ekonomiki*, No. 5, May 1966, p. 84; P. J. D. Wiles, *Communist International Economics*, Oxford 1968, p. 235.
[2] C. Simon, 'La planification en U.R.S.S. et en Europe Orientale: difficultés des plans 1980', *Etudes et Conjoncture*, 19e année, No. 4, April 1964, p. 60.

on a national basis and on the international CMEA level. The Eastern European studies reviewed above indicate considerable progress from the rudimentary *ad hoc* methods used in the first days of Soviet and Eastern European planning. On the other hand it has become clear that, unless the capacity of computers is very much increased, no adaptation of existing indicators or adoption of linear programming models can attain the results which could follow from a large degree of decentralization based on sweeping price reforms. Such developments would seem to be a part, if only a small one, of the general (not solely economic) reforms which the socialist societies are (or should be) introducing. And the urgent need for such reforms need not call into question the general socio-economic structure of the Eastern European countries; on the contrary, the reforms could help to implement the ideals this structure is intended to achieve: a faster growth of the material basis of society and a much greater real freedom for the individual. Dangers to the ideals of socialism may be associated with the re-establishment of such concepts as the profit motive (though such dangers, as has been shown, may be exaggerated),[1] but almost certainly greater dangers lie in store for socialism if the present system of administrative and irresponsible rule is continued, be it over the economic or the political life of the countries concerned.

[1] M. Ellman, 'Lessons of the Soviet Economic Reform', in R. Miliband and J. Saville (eds.), *The Socialist Register 1968*, London 1968.

APPENDIX

STATISTICAL TABLES

List of abbreviations for sources:

U.N., *N.A.*	United Nations, Yearbook of National Accounts Statistics
U.N., *T.S.*	United Nations, Yearbook of International Trade Statistics
U.N., *M.B.*	United Nations, Monthly Bulletin of Statistics
U.N., *S.Y.*	United Nations, Statistical Yearbook
U.N., *E.C.E.*	United Nations, Economic Commission for Europe

TABLE I. *Albania*

	National income		Imports: value (million leks)
	Volume indices		
	1950 = 100	1955 = 100 1960 prices	
1950	100	—	1,103
1951	—	—	1,978
1952	—	—	1,590
1953	—	—	2,001
1954	—	—	1,292
1955	170	100·0	2,141
1956	—	—	1,940
1957	—	—	2,666
1958	—	—	3,930
1959	—	—	4,265
1960	—	140·5	4,054
1961	—	150·5	3,612
1962	—	159·3	3,229
1963	—	175·8	3,537
1964	—	186·0	4,906
1965	—	186·5	—
1966	—	203·3	—
1967	—	218·5	—
1968	—	242·5	—
	Trend growth rates (percentages)		
1950–5	(11·2)		6·7
1955–60	(7·0)		18·5
1960–4	7·4		3·7
1964–8	7·1		—

SOURCES: National Income (1950–5): A. Nowicki, 'L'intégration économique des pays de l'Europe Orientale', *Cahiers de l'I.S.E.A.*, Série G (No. 22), No. 168, December 1965, p. 217; (1955–68): U.N., *N.A.* 1967; U.N., *E.C.E. Economic Survey of Europe in 1968*, New York 1969, p. 88. Imports: U.N., *T.S.*, 1966.

TABLE 2. *Bulgaria*

	National income		Imports	
	Volume indices		Value indices 1950 = 100	F.o.b. value (million leva)
	1950 = 100 1939 prices	1958 = 100 1958 prices		
1950	100	—	100	—
1951	128	—	93	—
1952	124	—	112	—
1953	154	—	145	—
1954	150	—	147	—
1955	171	82	138	292·4
1956	—	83	—	293·8
1957	—	94	—	388·6
1958	—	100	—	428·9
1959	—	122	—	677·9
1960	—	130	—	740·1
1961	—	134	—	779·2
1962	—	142	—	918·1
1963	—	153	—	1,091·9
1964	—	168	—	1,243·0
1965	—	180	—	1,377·9
1966	—	200	—	1,729·6
1967	—	218	—	1,839
1968	—	232	—	2,058

Trend growth rates
(percentages)

1950–5	10·1	9·7
1955–60	10·6	23·0
1960–4	6·7	14·7
1964–8	8·7	13·9

SOURCES: National Income (1950–5): U.N., *E.C.E.*, *Economic Survey of Europe in 1957*, Geneva 1958, p. A 66; (1955–68): U.N., *N.A.*, 1966 and 1967: U.N., *E.C.E.*, *Economic Survey of Europe in 1968*, New York 1969, p. 172. Imports (1950–5): U.N., *E.C.E.*, *Economic Survey of Europe in 1957*, Geneva 1958, p. A 66; (1955–68): U.N., *T.S.* 1966 and U.N., *M.B.*, August 1969.

TABLE 3. *Czechoslovakia*

	National income		Imports F.o.b. value (million koruna)
	Volume indices 1950 = 100 1955 prices	Billion koruna 1960 prices	
1950	100	—	4,603
1951	110	—	6,456
1952	121	—	6,307
1953	129	—	6,330
1954	134	—	6,716
1955	147	—	7,579
1956	155	—	8,537
1957	166	—	9,985
1958	180	—	9,772
1959	192	—	11,537
1960	207	162·0	13,072
1961	—	173·0	14,570
1962	—	175·4	14,904
1963	—	171·6	15,554
1964	—	172·6	17,488
1965	—	178·5	19,242
1966	—	196·7	19,699
1967	—	210·3	19,296
1968	—	225·0	22,425
	Trend growth rates (percentages)		
1950–5	7·7		7·8
1955–60	7·2		10·9
1960–4	1·2		6·7
1964–8	7·2		5·1

SOURCES: National Income: U.N., *N.A.*, 1958, 1959, 1963 and 1967; U.N., E.C.E., *Economic Survey of Europe in 1968*, New York 1969, p. 172. Imports: U.N., *T.S.*, 1966 and U.N., *M.B.*, August 1969.

TABLE 4. *DDR*

	National income Volume indices 1955 = 100 1963 prices	Imports[a] F.o.b. value (million valuta-marks)
1950	—	1,973
1951	1950 to 1955,	2,554
1952	+ 10·2%	3,248
1953	per annum	4,130
1954	—	4,607
1955	100	4,925
1956	107	5,605
1957	116	6,785
1958	129	7,143
1959	141	8,448
1960	147	9,217
1961	152	9,453
1962	156	10,111
1963	156	9,788
1964	163	11,061
1965	173	11,800
1966	182	13,503
1967	193	13,771
1968	203	14,229
	Trend growth rates (percentages)	
1950–5	(10·2)	20·7
1955–60	8·5	13·5
1960–4	2·4	4·1
1964–8	5·6	7·0

[a] Includes trade with West Germany.

SOURCES: National Income (1950–5): F. L. Pryor, *The Communist Foreign Trade System*, London 1963, p. 283; (1955–68): U.N., *N.A.* 1966 and 1967: U.N., E.C.E., *Economic Survey of Europe in 1968*, New York 1969, p. 172. Imports: U.N., *T.S.* 1966 and U.N., *M.B.*, August 1969.

TABLE 5. *Hungary*

	National income Volume indices		Imports C.i.f. value (million exchange forints)
	1954 = 100	1960 = 100 1959 prices	
1950	80·3	—	3,706
1951	93·9	—	4,626
1952	92·2	—	5,394
1953	104·2	—	5,722
1954	100·0	—	6,241
1955	108·9	—	6,507
1956	97·1	—	5,649
1957	119·7	—	8,011
1958	127·2	—	7,407
1959	136·0	—	9,309
1960	149·8	100·0	11,455
1961	—	106·1	12,040
1962	—	111·1	13,485
1963	—	117·5	15,327
1964	—	123·0	17,546
1965	—	124·4	17,849
1966	—	134·9	18,379
1967	—	146·6	20,841
1968	—	153·9	21,163
	Trend growth rates (percentages)		
1950–5	5·4		11·4
1955–60	7·9		12·9
1960–4	5·3		11·6
1964–8	6·3		5·5

SOURCES: National Income: U.N., *N.A.* 1957, 1963 and 1967; U.N., *E.C.E.*, *Economic Survey of Europe in 1968*, New York 1969, p. 172. Imports: U.N., *T.S.*, 1966 and U.N., *M.B.*, August 1969.

TABLE 6. *Poland*

	National income		Imports F.o.b. value (million exchange zlotys)
	Volume indices 1950 = 100 1950 prices	Billion zlotys 1961 prices	
1950	100	—	2,673
1951	104	—	3,697
1952	108	—	3,452
1953	124	—	3,097
1954	134	—	3,615
1955	146	276·5	3,727
1956	—	296·0	4,087
1957	—	327·8	5,006
1958	—	345·8	4,907
1959	—	363·9	5,678
1960	—	379·7	5,980
1961	—	410·7	6,747
1962	—	419·3	7,542
1963	—	448·4	7,916
1964	—	478·7	8,289
1965	—	512·2	9,361
1966	—	549·1	9,976
1967	—	579·8	10,579
1968	—	626·2	11,412
	Trend growth rates (percentages)		
1950–5	8·3		4·3
1955–60	6·7		10·0
1960–4	5·7		8·5
1964–8	6·8		7·9

SOURCES: National Income (1950–5): U.N., *E.C.E.*, *Economic Survey of Europe in 1957*, Geneva 1958, p. A 66; (1955–68): U.N., *N.A.* 1966 and 1967; U.N., *E.C.E.*, *Economic Survey of Europe in 1967*, New York 1968, Ch. 2, p. 3; and *Economic Survey of Europe in 1968*, New York 1969, p. 172. Imports: U.N., *T.S.* 1966 and U.N., *M.B.*, August 1969.

TABLE 7. *Rumania*

	National income Volume indices 1950 = 100 1950 prices	Imports F.o.b. value (million lei (for. curr.))	
1950	100	1,460	—
1951	131	1,636	—
1952	137	1,996	—
1953	158	2,340	—
1954	157	2,062	—
1955	192	2,335	2,771
1956	178	—	(2,500)
1957	207	—	(3,050)
1958	214	—	2,890
1959	242	—	3,012
1960	268	—	3,887
1961	295	—	4,888
1962	308	—	5,647
1963	338	—	6,132
1964	377	—	7,009
1965	413	—	6,463
1966	454	—	7,279
1967	486	—	9,276
1968	520	—	9,654

Trend growth rates (percentages)

1950–5	11·9	9·6
1955–60	7·8	6·5
1960–4	8·5	15·1
1964–8	8·4	10·5

SOURCES: National Income: U.N., *N.A.* 1958, 1963 and 1967; U.N., *E.C.E.*, *Economic Survey of Europe in 1968*, New York 1969, p. 172. Imports (1950–5): J. M. Montias, *Economic Development in Communist Rumania*, Cambridge, Mass. 1967, p. 137; (1958–66): ibid.; (1966–8): U.N., *M.B.*, August 1969; (1956–7): tentative estimates.

TABLE 8. *Soviet Union*

	National income Volume indices		Imports F.o.b. value (million roubles)
	1950 = 100	1958 = 100 1958 prices	
1950	100	—	1,310
1951	—	—	1,792
1952	—	—	2,256
1953	—	—	2,492
1954	—	—	2,864
1955	171	75	2,755
1956	—	83	3,251
1957	—	89	3,544
1958	—	100	3,915
1959	—	108	4,566
1960	—	116	5,066
1961	—	124	5,245
1962	—	131	5,810
1963	—	136	6,353
1964	—	149	6,963
1965	—	159	7,252
1966	—	172	7,122
1967	—	187	7,683
1968	—	201	8,469
	Trend growth rates (percentages)		
1950–5	(11·3)		16·1
1955–60	9·2		12·6
1960–4	6·1		8·6
1964–8	7·9		4·6

SOURCES: National Income (1950–5): O. Bogomolov, *Ekonomicheskaya effektivnost mezhdunarodnogo sotsialisticheskogo razdelenie truda*, Moscow 1965, p. 133; (1955–68); U.N., *N.A.* 1966 and 1967; U.N., *E.C.E.*, *Economic Survey of Europe in 1968*, New York 1969, p. 89. Imports: U.N., *T.S.* 1966 and U.N., *M.B.*, August 1969.

TABLE 9. *Total CMEA exports*
F.o.b. value (US $ millions)

| | Total exports | | | CMEA's share | |
	Including intra-German trade	Excluding intra-German trade	Exports to CMEA[a]	including	excluding
				intra-German trade	
1938	—	1,960	198	—	1·0
1948	—	3,170	1,405	—	44·3
1950	4,220	4,140	2,535	60·1	61·2
1951	5,375	5,340	3,240	60·3	60·7
1952	6,100	6,070	3,750	61·5	61·8
1953	6,850	6,780	4,340	63·4	64·0
1954	7,505	7,400	4,650	62·0	62·8
1955	8,085	7,950	4,750	58·8	59·7
1956	8,595	8,440	4,830	56·2	57·2
1957	9,805	9,600	5,930	60·5	61·8
1958	10,320	10,110	6,060	58·7	59·9
1959	12,220	11,990	7,390	60·5	61·6
1960	13,210	12,970	8,080	61·2	62·3
1961	14,340	14,120	8,970	62·6	63·5
1962	15,980	15,770	10,170	63·6	64·5
1963	17,245	17,000	11,030	64·0	64·9
1964	18,665	18,400	11,960	64·1	65·0
1965	20,005	19,710	12,460	62·3	63·2
1966	21,215	20,910	12,540	59·1	60·0
1967	23,120	22,820	13,740	59·4	60·2
1968	25,335	25,000	15,220	60·1	60·9
	Annual averages				
1950–5	6,360	6,280	3,880	61·0	61·8
1955–60	10,370	10,180	6,170	59·5	60·6
1960–4	15,890	15,650	10,040	63·2	64·2
1964–8	21,670	21,370	13,180	60·8	61·7

[a] Including Albania and excluding Mongolia.

SOURCES: (1938–1950): U.N., *S.Y.* 1960; (1951–7): U.N., *S.Y.* 1961; (1958–67): U.N., *S.Y.* 1968; (1968): U.N., *M.B.* June 1969.

BIBLIOGRAPHY

A. BOOKS

Agoston, I., *Le Marché Commun Communiste*, Paris 1965.

Alton, T. P., *Polish post-war Economy*, New York 1955.

Balassa, B. A., *The Hungarian Experience in Economic Planning*, New Haven 1959.

Bergson, A., *The Economics of Soviet Planning*, New Haven 1964.

Berliner, J. S., *Soviet Economic Aid*, New York 1958.

Bettelheim, Ch., *Studies in the Theory of Planning*, Asia Publishing House 1959.

Bogomolov, O. (ed.), *Ekonomicheskaya effektivnost mezhdunarodnogo sotsialisticheskogo rasdelenie truda*, Moscow 1965.

Boltho, A., *An Examination of Foreign Trade Criteria in Socialist Economies*, Unpublished B.Litt. Dissertation, Oxford University 1967.

Brown, A. A. and Neuberger, E. (eds.), *International Trade and Central Planning*, Berkeley and Los Angeles 1968.

Caves, R. E., *Trade and Economic Structure*, Cambridge, Mass. 1960.

Chambre, H., *Le Marxisme en Union Soviétique*, Paris 1955.

Chervyakov, P. A., *Organisatsiya i technika vneshnyei torgovli S.S.S.R.*, Moscow 1962.

Csikos-Nagy, B., *Pricing in Hungary*, London 1968.

Dewar, M., *Soviet Trade with Eastern Europe, 1945–1949*, London 1951.

Dickinson, H. D., *Economics of Socialism*, Oxford 1939.

Dobb, M., *On Economic Theory and Socialism*, London 1955.

An Essay on Economic Growth and Planning, London 1960.

Soviet Economic Development since 1917, London 1966.

Welfare Economics and the Economics of Socialism, Cambridge 1969.

Eidel'man, M. R., *Statistika materialno-technichesko snabzheniya*, Moscow 1953.

Engels, F., *Anti-Dühring*, Moscow 1959.

Erlich, A., *The Soviet Industrialization Debate, 1924–1928*, Cambridge, Mass. 1960.

Grepsov, G. I. and Karpov, P. P. (eds.), *Material'nyie balansi v narodnokhozyaistvennom plane*, Moscow 1960.

Haberler, G., *International Trade and Economic Development*, Cairo 1959.

von Hayek, F. A. (ed.), *Collectivist Economic Planning*, London 1938.

Hermes, T., *Der Aussenhandel in den Ostblockstaaten*, Hamburg 1958.

Hirsch, H., *Mengenplanung und Preisplanung in der Sowjetunion*, Tübingen 1957.

Institut Mezhdunarodnich Otnoshenyi (Institute for International Relations), *Organisatsiya i technika vneshnyei torgovli S.S.S.R. i drugich sotsialisticheskich stran*, Moscow 1963.

Johnson, H. G., *International Trade and Economic Growth*, London 1958.

Kaser, M. C., *Comecon* (2nd edition), London 1967.

Kindleberger, C. P., *International Economics*, Homewood, Ill. 1958.

Foreign Trade and the National Economy, New Haven 1962.

Klinkmüller, E., *Die gegenwärtige Aussenhandelsverflechtung der Sowjetischen Besatzungszone Deutschlands*, Berlin 1959.

Köhler, H., *Economic Integration in the Soviet Bloc: with an East German Case Study*, New York 1965.

Kohlmey, G., *Der demokratische Weltmarkt*, Berlin 1956.

Lerner, A. P., *The Economics of Control*, New York 1944.

Little, I. M. D., *A Critique of Welfare Economics*, Oxford 1960.

Lockwood, W. W., *The Economic Development of Japan*, Princeton 1954.

Luzzatto, G., *L'economia italiana dal 1861 al 1894*, Torino 1968.

Maddison, A., *Economic Growth in Japan and the USSR*, London 1969.

Mandel, E., *Traité d'économie Marxiste*, Paris 1962.

Marczewski, J., *Planification et croissance économique des démocraties populaires*, Paris 1956.

Marx, K., *Critique of the Gotha Programme*, London 1933.

A Contribution to the Critique of Political Economy, Chicago 1913.

Capital, Moscow 1961.

Gründrisse der Kritik der Politischen Ökonomie, Berlin 1953.

Mateev, E., *Mezhdunarodnoe sotsialisticheskoe rasdelenie truda i narodnokhozyaistvennoe planirovanye*, Moscow 1965.

Meade, J. E., *The Theory of Customs Union*, Amsterdam 1955.

Meek, R. L., *Studies in the Labour Theory of Value*, London 1956.

Mervart, J., *Vyznam a vyvojcem v mezinarodnim obchode* (English summary), Prague 1960.

Montias, J. M., *Central Planning in Poland*, New Haven 1962.

Economic Development in Communist Rumania, Cambridge, Mass. 1967.

Nove, A., *The Soviet Economy*, London 1961.

Nove, A. and Donnelly, D., *Trade with Communist Countries*, London 1960.

Pareto, V., *Cours d'économie politique*, Paris 1964.

Popovic, M., *On Economic Relations among Socialist Countries*, London 1950.

Preobrazhensky, E., *La nouvelle économique* (translated by B. Joly), Paris 1966.

Pryor, F. L., *The Communist Foreign Trade System*, London 1963.

Rakowski, M., *Efficiency of Investment in a Socialist Economy*, Oxford 1966.

Robinson, J., *An Essay on Marxian Economics*, London 1947.

Schumpeter, J., *History of Economic Analysis*, London 1955.

Schwartz, H., *Russia's Soviet Economy*, London 1957.

Shagalov, G., *Ekonomicheskaya effektivnost tovarnogo obmena mezhdu sotsialisticheskimi stranami*, Moscow 1966.

Sik, O., *Plan and Market under Socialism*, Prague 1967.

Spulber, N., *The Economics of Communist Eastern Europe*, New York 1957.
Soviet Strategy for Economic Growth, Bloomington, Indiana 1964.
(ed.), *Foundations of Soviet Strategy for Economic Growth: Selected Soviet Essays, 1924–1930*, Bloomington, Indiana 1964.

Stalin, J., *Economic Problems of Socialism in the U.S.S.R.*, Moscow 1952.

Sweezy, P. M., *The Theory of Capitalist Development*, London 1946.
Socialism, New York 1949.

Tinbergen, J., *International Economic Co-operation*, Amsterdam 1945.

Vajda, I., *The Role of Foreign Trade in a Socialist Economy*, Budapest 1965.

Viner, J., *Studies in the Theory of International Trade*, London 1937.
The Customs Union Issue, New York 1950.

Waterston, A., *Planning in Yugoslavia*, I.B.R.D., Baltimore 1962.

Wiles, P. J. D., *Price, Cost and Output*, Oxford 1956.
The Political Economy of Communism, Oxford 1962.
Communist International Economics, Oxford 1968.

Zauberman, A., *Industrial Progress in Poland, Czechoslovakia and East Germany—1937–1962*, London 1964.
Aspects of Planometrics, London 1967.

Zsoldos, L., *The Economic Integration of Hungary in the Soviet Bloc: Foreign Trade Experience*, Columbus, Ohio 1963.

B. ARTICLES

List of abbreviations:

A.E.R.	The American Economic Review
Auss.	Der Aussenhandel
Cahiers de l'I.S.E.A.	Cahiers de l'Institut de Science Economique Appliquée
C.E.P.	Czechoslovak Economic Papers
E.J.	The Economic Journal
E.P.	Economics of Planning
P.K.	Planovoe Khozyaistvo
R.E.	The Review of Economic Studies

R.E.S.   The Review of Economics and Statistics
S.S.   Soviet Studies
V.E.   Voprosy Ekonomiki
V.T.   Vneshnyaya Torgovlya
W.W.   Wirtschaftswissenschaft
B. & N.   A. A. Brown and E. Neuberger (eds.), *International Trade and Central Planning*, Berkeley and Los Angeles 1968.

Adler-Karlsson, G., 'The Semi-developed Soviet Economy—A Foreign Trade Illustration', *E.P.* Vol. VI, No. 1, 1966.
'Some notes on the Foreign Trade Decisions in the U.S.S.R.', *Øst Økonomi*, No. 3–4, 1961.
Aizenberg, I., 'Ekonomicheskye predposilki povishenya roli Rublya v mezhdunarodnich rastchetach', *Dengi i Kredit*, No. 4, April 1962.
Ames, E., 'The Exchange Rate in Soviet-type Economies', *R.E.S.* Vol. XXXV, No. 4, November 1953.
'International Trade without Markets—The Soviet Bloc Case', *A.E.R.* Vol. XLIV, No. 5, December 1954.
Anonymous, 'Teaching of Economics in the Soviet Union', translated from the Russian (*Pod Znamenem Marxisma*, No. 7–8, 1943) in *A.E.R.* Vol. XXXIV, No. 3, September 1944.
Introduction to W. Trzeciakowski, 'Model tekuschchei optimisatsyi vneshnyei torgovli i ee primenenie', *V.T.* No. 6, June 1964.
Appenfelder, G. and Sydow, P., 'Zu praktischen Problemen bei der Optimierung der Regionalstruktur gegenüber kapitalistischen Ländern', *Auss.* No. 5, May 1964.
Balassa, B., 'Planning in an Open Economy', *Kyklos*, Vol. XIX, No. 3, 1966.
Balaszy, S., 'Aktualnye voprosy opredelenya effektivnosti vneshnyei torgovli', *P.K.* No. 8, August 1962.
'Rational Foreign Trade Decisions in a Planned Economy on the basis of Correct Prices and Rates of Exchange', *Mimeo*, March 1965.
'Der Aussenhandel und die Reform der Wirtschaftsführung in der Ungarischen Volksrepublik', *W.W.* No. 11, November 1967.
Barone, E., 'The Ministry of Production in the Collectivist State', translated from the Italian (*Giornale degli Economisti e Rivista di Statistica*, September–October 1908) in F. A. von Hayek (ed.), *Collectivist Economic Planning*, London 1938.
Beckerman, W., 'Projecting Europe's Growth', *E.J.* Vol. LXXII, No. 288, December 1962.

Bergson, A., 'Market Socialism Revisited', *The Journal of Political Economy*, Vol. LXXV, No. 5, October 1967.

Bogomolov, O., 'O mezhdunarodnom sotsialisticheskom rasdelenya truda', *Mirovaiya Ekonomika i Mezhdunarodnoe Otnosheniya*, No. 4, April 1959.

'Mezhdunarodnoe sotsialisticheskoe rasdelenya truda', *V.E.* No. 1, January 1960.

'Metodologitcheskye problemi mezhdunarodnogo sotsialisticheskogo rasdelenya truda', *V.E.* No. 11, November 1963.

Borisenko, A., 'K voprosu ob effektivnosti sotsialisticheskoi vnesh-nyei torgovli', *V.T.* No. 10, October 1964.

Borisenko, A. and Shastitko, V., 'Voprosy ekonomicheskoi effektiv-nosti vneshnyei torgovli v sotsialisticheskich stranach', *V.T.* No. 5, May 1962.

Bornstein, M., 'The Reform and Revaluation of the Ruble', *A.E.R.* Vol. LI, No. 1, March 1961.

'The Soviet Price System', *A.E.R.* Vol. LII, No. 1, March 1962.

'The Soviet Price Reform Discussion', *The Quarterly Journal of Economics*, Vol. LXXVIII, No. 1, February 1964.

'Ideology and the Soviet Economy', *S.S.* Vol. XVIII, No. 1, July 1966.

Brauer, R., 'Zur Frage des Volkswirtschaftlichen Nutzeffekts des Aussenhandels', *W.W.* No. 3, March 1958.

Brown, A. A., 'Centrally Planned Foreign Trade and Economic Efficiency', *The American Economist*, Vol. V, No. 2, November 1962.

'Towards a Theory of Centrally Planned Foreign Trade', *B. & N.*

Brus, W., 'Sul ruolo della Legge del Valore nell'Economia Socialista', *Vecchia e Nuova Pianificazione Economica in Polonia*, Milan 1960.

'The Law of Value and the Market Mechanism in a Socialist Economy', *Problems of Economic Theory and Practice in Poland— Studies on the Theory of Reproduction and Prices*, Warsaw 1964.

Brus, W. and Laski, K., 'The Law of Value and the Problem of Allocation in Socialism', *On Political Economy and Econometrics— Essays in honour of Oskar Lange*, Warsaw 1964.

'Problems of the Theory of Growth under Socialism', in E. A. G. Robinson (ed.), *Problems in Economic Development*, London 1965.

Caiola, M., 'Balance of Payments of the U.S.S.R., 1955–58', *International Monetary Fund Staff Papers*, Vol. IX, No. 1, March 1962.

'Balance of Payments of the U.S.S.R., 1959–60', *International Monetary Fund Staff Papers*, Vol. X, No. 2, July 1963.

Cerniansky, V., 'Die Preisbasis auf dem sozialistischen Weltmarkt', *Auss.* No. 4–5, March 1958.

'Problems of the Economic Efficiency of Foreign Trade', *C.E.P.* No. 1, Prague 1959.

Chambre, H., 'La doctrine Soviétique concernant les pays du "Tiers Monde"', *Cahiers de l'I.S.E.A.*, Série G (No. 13), No. 124, April 1962.

Chaudhuri, M. K., 'Problems of Perspective Planning in the German Democratic Republic', *E.P.* Vol. iv, No. 2, 1964.

Chenery, H. B., 'Comparative Advantage and Economic Development', *A.E.R.* Vol. li, No. 1, March 1961.

Colette, J. M., 'Le blocage de la croissance économique tchécoslovaque', *Cahiers de l'I.S.E.A.*, Série G (No. 22), No. 168, December 1965.

Cukor, G., 'Use of Input-Output Tables in Long-term Planning of the Relations between Industry and Foreign Trade', in O. Lukacs (ed.), *Input-Output Tables—Their Compilation and Use*, Budapest 1962.

Deutsch, K. W. and Eckstein, A., 'National Industrialization and the Declining Share of the International Economic Sector, 1890–1959', *World Politics*, Vol. xiii, No. 2, January 1961.

Dickinson, H. D., Notes to article by L. Johansen, 'Labour Theory of Value and Marginal Utilities', *E.P.* Vol. iii, No. 3, December 1963.

Domar, E. D., 'A Soviet Model of Growth', in E. D. Domar, *Essays in the Theory of Economic Growth*, New York 1957.

Review of E. Preobrazhensky, 'The New Economics', *S.S.* Vol. xviii, No. 2, October 1966.

Dudinskii, I., 'Nekotorye tcherti rasvitya mirovogo sotsialisticheskogo rinka', *V.E.* No. 2, February 1961.

Eckstein, A., 'Foreign Trade of China: A Summary Appraisal', *B. & N.*

Ellman, M., 'Lessons of the Soviet Economic Reform', in R. Miliband and J. Saville (eds.), *The Socialist Register 1968*, London 1968.

Fiszel, H., 'The Calculation of the Economic Efficiency of Foreign Trade', in *On Political Economy and Econometrics—Essays in honour of Oskar Lange*, Warsaw 1964.

Fomin, B. S., Davidovich, D. Z. and Aleinikov, B. I., 'K analisu vneshnyei torgovli v optimalnom plane', *Ekonomika i Matematicheskyi Metody*, Vol. ii, No. 5, September–October 1966.

Frumkin, A., 'Nesostayatelnost burzhuaznoi teorii vneshnyei torgovli', *V.E.* No. 12, December 1959.

Galeson, W., 'Economic Relations between the Soviet Union and Communist China', in N. Spulber (ed.), *Study of the Soviet Economy*, Bloomington, Indiana 1961.

Gatovski, L., 'Ob ispol'sovanyi zakona stoimosti v sotsialisticheskom khozyaistve', *Kommunist*, No. 9, June 1957.

Gehrels, F. and Johnston, B. F., 'The Economic Gains of European Integration', *The Journal of Political Economy*, Vol. LXIII, No. 4, August 1955.

Georgiev, E., 'Ekonomika sotsialisticheskoi vneshnyei torgovli', *V.T.* No. 5, May 1963.

'Voprosy effektivnosti i rentabelnosti', *V.T.* No. 7, July 1964.

Glickman, P., 'Ob effektivnosti spetsialisatsyi i kooperirovanya proisvodstva stran chlenov SEV', *V.E.* No. 2, February 1967.

Glowacki, J., 'Optimizing the Direction of International Trade in a Planned Economy', *E.P.* Vol. VI, No. 1, 1966.

Goldmann, J. and Flek, J., 'Economic Growth in Czechoslovakia', *E.P.* Vol. VI, No. 2, 1966.

Gollmer, K., 'Optimierung der Exportrentabilität', *Auss.* No. 6, June 1963.

Göncöl, G., 'A propos de la théorie marxiste du commerce extérieur', translated from the Hungarian (*Közgazdasagi Szemle*, No. 11, 1955) in *Etudes Economiques*, No. 95–6, 1956.

Grote, G., 'Zur Anwendung matematischer Methoden bei der Planung und Leitung des Aussenhandels', *Auss.* No. 3, March 1963.

Haberler, G., 'Theoretical Reflexions on the Trade of Socialist Economies', *B. & N.*

Hamouz, F., 'Foreign Trade under the New System of Planned Management', translated from the Czech (*Nova Mysl*, No. 1, 1964), in *American Review of Soviet and Eastern European Foreign Trade*, Vol. I, No. 6, November–December 1965.

Heckscher, E., 'The Effect of Foreign Trade on the Distribution of Income', translated from the Swedish (*Ekonomisk Tidskrift*, Vol. XXI, 1919) in The American Economic Association, *Readings in the Theory of International Trade*, London 1950.

Hecht, C., 'Methoden und Kennziffern zur Ermittlung des Nutzeffektes der sozialistischen internationale Arbeitsteilung', *Auss.* No. 7, July 1964 and No. 8, August 1964.

Hoeffding, O., 'Recent Structural Changes and Balance-of-Payments Adjustments in Soviet Foreign Trade', *B. & N.*

Holzman, F. D., 'Some Financial Aspects of Soviet Foreign Trade', in Joint Economic Committee, Congress of the United States, *Comparisons of the United States and Soviet Economies*, Washington 1959.

'Soviet Foreign Trade Pricing and the question of Discrimination: A "Customs Union" Approach', *R.E.S.* Vol. xliv, No. 2, May 1962.

'Foreign Trade' in A. Bergson and S. Kuznets (eds.), *Economic Trends in the Soviet Union*, Cambridge, Mass. 1963.

'Background and Origin of the Rumanian Dispute with Comecon', *S.S.* Vol. xvi, No. 2, October 1964.

'More on Soviet Bloc Trade Discrimination', *S.S.* Vol. xvii, No. 1, July 1965.

'Soviet Central Planning and its Impact on Foreign Trade Behaviour and Adjustment Mechanisms', *B. & N.*

'The Ruble Exchange Rate and Soviet Foreign Trade Pricing Policies', *A.E.R.* Vol. lviii, No. 4, September 1968.

Horovitz, M., 'A propos de certaines particularités et de certaines limitations de la Loi de la Valeur dans le commerce extérieur socialiste', translated from the Rumanian (Probleme Economice, No. 4, 1958) in *Etudes Economiques*, No. 112–13, 1958.

Hoselitz, B. F., 'Socialist Planning and International Economic Relations', *A.E.R.* Vol. xxxiii, No. 4, December 1943.

Hurwicz, L., 'Conditions for Economic Efficiency of Centralized and Decentralized Economic Structures', in G. Grossman (ed.), *Value and Plan*, Berkeley and Los Angeles 1960.

Jasay, A. E., 'Criteria for Foreign Trading Decisions with Arbitrary Home Prices', *Mimeo*, July 1958.

Kaigl, V., 'International Division of Labour in the World Socialist System', *C.E.P.* No. 1, Prague 1959.

Kamecki, Z. J., 'The Problems of Foreign Trade Monopoly in a Socialist Economy', in J. Soldaczuk (ed.), *International Trade and Development—Theory and Policy*, Warsaw 1966.

Karady, G., 'Calculation of the Economic Character of Foreign Trade', translated excerpts from the Hungarian (*Közgazdasagi Szemle*, No. 2, 1959) in L. Zsoldos, *The Economic Integration of Hungary into the Soviet Bloc: Foreign Trade Experience*, Columbus, Ohio 1963.

Khachaturov, T., 'Opredelenye effektivnosti kapitalnich vlozhenyi v stranach S.E.V.', *V.E.* No. 7, July 1964.

Knisiak, S., 'The Economic Criteria of the International Specialization of Production in Socialist Countries', *Mimeo*, 1964.

Kohlmey, G., 'Karl Marx' Theorie von den internationalen Werten', *Probleme der Politischen Ökonomie*, Berlin 1962.

'Wirtschaftswachstum und Aussenhandel', *Auss.* No. 3, March 1965.

'From Extensive to Intensive Economic Growth', *C.E.P.* No. 6, Prague 1966.

'Karl Marx' Aussenhandelstheorie und Probleme der aussen-wirtschaftlichen Beziehungen zwischen sozialistischen Staaten', *W.W.* No. 8., August 1967.

Konius, A. A., 'Raschirenie sistemi uravnenyi mezhotraslovich sviasei dlya tselei perspektivnogo planirovanya', in V. Nemchinov (ed.), *Primenenie matematiki v ekonomicheskich isledovanyach*, Moscow 1961.

Kornai, J., 'Mathematical Programming of Long-term Plans in Hungary', *Mimeo*, June 1963.

'Two-level Planning', *Mimeo*, May 1964.

'Mathematical Programming as a tool in drawing up the Five-Year Economic Plan', *E.P.* Vol. v, No. 3, 1965.

Kornai, J. and Liptak, T., 'Two-level Planning', *Econometrica*, Vol. xxxiii, No. 1, January 1965.

Kornai, J. and Martos, B., 'The Application of the Input-Output Table to determine the optimum Development Program of the Aluminium Industry', in O. Lukacs (ed.), *Input-Output Tables—Their Compilation and Use*, Budapest 1962.

von Krepl, K. and Gollmer, K., 'Erfahrungen des A.H.U. Invest Export bei der Optimierung zusammenhängender Warengruppen des Maschinenbaus', *Auss.* No. 6, June 1965.

Kronrod, Y. A., 'Stoimost kak basa tseni v uslovyach sotsialisticheskoi ekonomiki', *V.E.* No. 10, October 1960.

Kronsjö, T., 'Iterative Pricing for Planning Foreign Trade', *E.P.* Vol. iii, No. 1, April 1963.

Ladigin, B. and Shiraev, Y., 'Voprosy sovershenstvovaniya ekonomicheskogo sotrudnichestva stran SEV', *V.E.* No. 5, May 1966.

Lange, O., 'Marxian Economics and Modern Economic Theory', *R.E.* Vol. ii, No. 3, June 1935.

'Role of Planning in Socialist Economy', in O. Lange (ed.), *Problems of Political Economy of Socialism*, New Delhi 1962.

Lange, O. and Taylor, F. M., 'On the Economic Theory of Socialism', in B. E. Lippincott (ed.), *On the Economic Theory of Socialism*, University of Minnesota 1938.

Leontief, W., 'Domestic Production and Foreign Trade; the American Capital Position Re-examined', in R. E. Caves and H. G. Johnson (eds.), *Readings in International Economics*, London 1968.

Lerner, A. P., 'Economic Theory and Socialist Economy', *R.E.* Vol. ii, No. 1, October 1934.

'A Note on Socialist Economics', *R.E.* Vol. iv, No. 1, October 1936.

'Statics and Dynamics in Socialist Economics', *E.J.* Vol. xlvii, No. 186, June 1937.

Lesz, M., 'The Effectiveness of Investment and the Optimization of a Long-term Plan', translated from the Polish (*Gospodarka*

Planowa, No. 6, 1964), in *Mathematical Studies in Economics and Statistics in the USSR and Eastern Europe*, Vol. I, No. 1, Fall 1964.

Levine, H. S., 'The Centralized Planning of Supply in Soviet Industry', in M. Bornstein and D. R. Fusfeld (eds.), *The Soviet Economy—A Book of Readings*, Homewood, Ill. 1962.

'Input-Output Analysis and Soviet Planning', *A.E.R.* Vol. LII, No. 2 (Papers and Proceedings), May 1962.

'The Effects of Foreign Trade on Soviet Planning Practices', *B. & N.*

Lipsey, R. G.,'The Theory of Customs Unions: A General Survey', in R. E. Caves and H. G. Johnson (eds.), *Readings in International Economics*, London 1968.

Liska, T. and Marias, A., 'Optimum Returns and International Division of Labour', translated excerpts from the Hungarian (*Közgazdasagi Szemle*, No. 1, 1954) in: United Nations, Economic Commission for Europe, *Economic Survey of Europe in 1954*, Geneva 1955.

Maier, W. and Mann, H., 'Die Grosshandelspreise als Ausgangspunkt für die Schaffung einer eigenen Preisbasis im Handel zwischen den sozialistischen Ländern', *W.W.* No. 4, April 1964.

Maksimovic, I. M., 'Professor Oskar Lange on Economic Theory of Socialism and Yugoslav Economic Thinking', in: *On Political Economy and Econometrics—Essays in honour of Oskar Lange*, Warsaw 1964.

Malyshev, I., 'Nekotorye voprosy tsenoobrazovanya v sotsialisticheskom khozyaistve', *V.E.* No. 3, March 1957.

Manevich, E., 'Vseobshchnost truda i problemy ratsionalnogo ispolzovanyia rabochei sily v S.S.R.', *V.E.* No. 6, June 1965.

Marton, A. and Tardos, M., 'Short-run Optimization of the Commodity Pattern by Markets of Foreign Trade', *E.P.* Vol. IV, No. 2, 1964.

Mendershausen, H., 'Terms of Trade between the Soviet Union and the smaller Communist Countries, 1955–1957', *R.E.S.* Vol. XLI, No. 2, May 1959.

'The Terms of Soviet-Satellite Trade: A Broadened Analysis', *R.E.S.* Vol. XLII, No. 2, May 1960.

Mervart, J., 'The Significance of certain Problems of the Operation of the Law of Value on the World Socialist Market', *C.E.P.* No. 1, Prague 1959.

Mishan, E. J. and Zauberman, A., 'Resurrection of the Concept of Consumers' Choice', in A. Zauberman, *Aspects of Planometrics*, London 1967.

Montias, J. M., 'Planning with Material Balances in Soviet-type Economies', *A.E.R.* Vol. XLIX, No. 5, December 1959.

'Unbalanced Growth in Rumania', *A.E.R.* Vol. LIII, No. 2 (Papers and Proceedings), May 1963.

'Socialist Industrialization and Trade in Machinery Products', *B. & N.*

Morgan, J., 'Rumania stands firm', *New Statesman*, Vol. LXX, No. 1793, 23 July 1965.

Morishima, M. and Seton, F., 'Aggregation in Leontief Matrices and the Labour Theory of Value', *Econometrica*, Vol. XXIX, No. 2, April 1961.

Mycielski, J., Rey, K. and Trzeciakowski, W., 'Decomposition and Optimization of Short-run Planning in a Planned Economy', in T. Barna (ed.), *Structural Interdependence and Economic Development*, London 1963.

Myint, H., 'Infant Industry Arguments for Assistance to Industries in the Setting of Dynamic Trade Theory', in R. Harrod and D. Hague (eds.), *International Trade Theory in a Developing World*, London 1963.

Nachtigal, V., 'Extensity and Efficiency of Economic Growth in Czechoslovakia', *C.E.P.* No. 9, Prague 1967.

Nagy, A., 'Un modèle d'optimisation à court terme des exportations et son application', *Economie Appliquée*, Tome XVI, No. 3, 1963.

Nagy, A. and Liptak, T., 'A Short-run Optimization Model of Hungarian Cotton Fabric Exports', *E.P.* Vol. III, No. 2, September 1963.

Nemchinov, V., 'Stoimost i tsena pri sotsialisme', *V.E.* No. 12, December 1960.

Editorial preface to: L. V. Kantorovich, *The Best Use of Economic Resources*, Oxford 1965.

Nove, A., 'The Liberman Proposals', *Survey*, No. 47, April 1963.

Nowicki, A., 'Premiers contours d'une théorie du commerce extérieur dans un pays à économie planifiée—le cas des échanges commerciaux de la Pologne', *Cahiers de l'I.S.E.A.*, Série G (No. 13), No. 124, April 1962.

'L'intégration économique des pays de l'Europe Orientale', *Cahiers de l'I.S.E.A.*, Série G (No. 22), No. 168, December 1965.

Orlicek, Z., 'Erfahrungen bei der Effektivitätsuntersuchung der Warenstruktur des tschechoslowakschen Aussenhandels', *Auss.* No. 11, November 1964.

Otto, G., 'Optimierung der territorialen Struktur des Aussenhandels', *Auss.* No. 3, March 1963 and No. 6, June 1963.

'Probleme der Linearen Optimierung in der Aussenhandelspraxis', *Auss.* No. 3, March 1964.

'Internationale Konferenz über Fragen der Aussenhandelsrentabilität', *Auss.* No. 6, June 1964.

Pajestka, J., 'Certain Problems of "Profitability Calculations" in Foreign Trade', in J. Soldaczuk (ed.), *International Trade and Development—Theory and Policy*, Warsaw 1966.

Perkins, D. H., 'The International Impact on Chinese Central Planning', *B. & N.*

Probst, A., 'Ob opredelenyi ekonomicheskogo effekta vneshnyei torgovli', *P.K.* No. 11, November 1965.

Pryor, F. L., 'Foreign Trade Theory in the Communist Bloc', *S.S.* Vol. XIV, No. 1, July 1962.

Rubinshtein, G., 'Rasvitie Sovetskogo importa', *V.T.* No. 5, May 1960.

Rychetnik, K., 'Mathematical Economics in Czechoslovakia', *E.P.* Vol. IV, No. 1, 1964.

Saltiel, J. P., 'Commerce extérieur et industrialisation—L'expérience des années 1930–1931', *Cahiers de l'I.S.E.A.*, Série G (No. 13), No. 124, April 1962.

Samuelson, P. A., 'The Gains from International Trade', in The American Economic Association, *Readings in the Theory of International Trade*, London 1950.

Schulmeister, D., 'Zur Optimierung der Waren- und Regional-Struktur im Aussenhandel der D.D.R.', *Auss.* No. 6, June 1965.

Scitovsky, T., 'A Reconsideration of the Theory of Tariffs', in The American Economic Association, *Readings in the Theory of International Trade*, London 1950.

Scott, N., Review of P. A. Chervyakov: *Organisatsiya i technika vneshnyei torgovli S.S.S.R.*, *S.S.* Vol. X, No. 4, April 1959.

Serck-Hanssen, J., 'Input-Output Tables in the U.S.S.R. and Eastern Europe', *Øst Økonomi*, No. 2, July 1962.

Shagalov, G., 'O metodach opredelenya ekonomicheskoi effectivnosti vneshnyei torgovli v Polshe', *V.T.* No. 3, March 1962.

'Voprosy ekonomicheskoi effektivnosti vneshnyei torgovli', *Vestnik Moskoskogo Universiteta*, Series VIII, No. 5, September–October 1963.

'Ekonomicheskaya effektivnost vneshnyei torgovli sotsialisticheskich stran', *V.E.* No. 6, June 1965.

Shastitko, V., 'Metodi opredelenya ekonomicheskoi effektivnosti vneshnyei torgovli v G.D.R.', *V.T.* No. 1, January 1962.

Shaynin, L. B., 'Proportions of Exchange', *E.J.* Vol. LXX, No. 280, December 1960.

Sherman, H. J., 'Marxist Economics and Soviet Planning', *S.S.* Vol. XVIII, No. 2, October 1966.

Shuckstal, I., 'Ob opredelenyi ekonomicheskoi effektivnosti kapitalnich vlozhenyi v stranach-chlenach S.E.V.', *V.E.* No. 10, October 1961.

Sik, O., 'La gestion économique en Tchécoslovaquie', *Les Temps Modernes*, 20e année, No. 229, June 1965.

'Problems of the New System of Planned Management', *C.E.P.* No. 5, Prague 1965.

Simon, C., 'La Planification en U.R.S.S. et en Europe Orientale', *Etudes et Conjoncture*, 19e année, No. 4, April 1964.

Smirnov, G., Zotov, B. and Shagalov, G., 'Otzenka ekonomicheskoi effektivnosti vneshnyei torgovli', *P.K.* No. 8, August 1964.

Soldaczuk, J., 'Foreign Trade and Economic Growth in the Socialist Economy', in J. Soldaczuk (ed.), *International Trade and Development—Theory and Policy*, Warsaw 1966.

Spulber, N., 'The Dispute: Economic Relations among Socialist States and the Soviet "Model"', in V. L. Benes, R. F. Byrnes and N. Spulber (eds.), *The Second Soviet-Yugoslav Dispute*, Indiana University, 1959.

'The Soviet Bloc Foreign Trade System', in M. Bornstein and D. R. Fusfeld (eds.), *The Soviet Economy—A Book of Readings*, Homewood, Ill. 1962.

Staller, G. J., 'Patterns of Stability in Foreign Trade: OECD and COMECON: 1950–1963', *A.E.R.* Vol. LVII, No. 4, September 1967.

Stolper, W. F. and Samuelson, P. A., 'Protection and Real Wages', *R.E.* Vol. IX, November 1941.

Tauchman, J. and Novozamsky, J., 'The Nature of the International Division of Labour under Socialism', *C.E.P.* No. 11, Prague 1969.

Terekhov, V. and Shastitko, V., 'O metodike sravnenyi effektivnosti kapitalnich vlozhenyi v stranach-chlenach S.E.V.', *P.K.* No. 11, November 1961.

Tinbergen, J., 'Do Communist and Free Economies show a Converging Pattern?', *S.S.* Vol. XII, No. 4, August 1961.

Treml, V. G., 'Input-Output Analysis and Soviet Planning', in J. P. Hardt et al. (eds.), *Mathematics and Computers in Soviet Economic Planning*, New Haven 1967.

Trzeciakowski, W., Comments in O. Lukacs (ed.), *Input-Output Tables—Their Compilation and Use*, Budapest 1962.

'Die Kriterien der aktuellen Effektivität des Aussenhandels und die Planung', *Auss.* No. 3, March 1964 and No. 4, April 1964.

'Model tekuschchei optimisatsyi vneshnyei torgovli i ee primenenie', *V.T.* No. 6, June 1964.

Vajda, I., 'Probleme und Formen der Wirtschaftskooperation der sozialistischen Länder', *W.W.* No. 10, October 1964.

Wilczynski, J., 'The Theory of Comparative Costs and Centrally Planned Economies', *E.J.* Vol. LXXV, No. 297, March 1965.

Wiles, P. J. D., 'Changing Economic Thought in Poland', *Oxford Economic Papers*, Vol. IX, No. 2, June 1957.
'Foreign Trade of Eastern Europe: A Summary Appraisal', *B. & N.*
Zarev, K., 'Mezhdunarodnaya spetsialisatsiya proisvodstva i kompleksnoe rasvitie ekonomiki otdelnich sotsialisticheskich stran', *P.K.* No. 4, April 1964.
Zauberman, A. 'The Soviet Debate on the Law of Value and Price Formation', in G. Grossman (ed.), *Value and Plan*, Berkeley and Los Angeles 1960.
'New Winds in Soviet Planning', *S.S.* Vol. XII, No. 1, July 1960.
'The Soviet and Polish Quest for a Criterion of Investment Efficiency', *Economica*, Vol. XXIX, No. 115, August 1962.
'A note on the Soviet Inter-Industry Labour Input Balance', *S.S.* Vol. XV. No. 1, July 1963.
'The Criterion of Efficiency of Foreign Trade in Soviet-type Economies', *Economica*, Vol. XXXI, No. 121, February 1964.
'On the Objective Function for the Soviet Economy', *Economica*, Vol. XXXII, No. 127, August 1965.

C. OTHER SOURCES

Council for Mutual Economic Assistance (CMEA), *Basic Principles of International Socialist Division of Labour*, quoted in M. C. Kaser, *Comecon* (2nd edition), London 1967.
Organization for Economic Co-operation and Development (OECD), *Economic Growth, 1960–1970*, Paris 1966.
United Nations, *Towards a New Trade Policy for Development* (Report by the Secretary General of the United Nations Conference on Trade and Development), New York 1964.
Planning for Economic Development, New York 1965.
Statistical Yearbook.
Yearbook of National Accounts Statistics.
Yearbook of International Trade Statistics.
Monthly Bulletin of Statistics.
United Nations, Economic Commission for Europe, *Economic Survey of Europe* (years 1954, 1957, 1960, 1961, 1962, 1964, 1965, 1966, 1967, 1968).
Economic Bulletin for Europe (Vol. XI, No. 1, June 1959 and No. 3, November 1959; Vol. XVI, No. 2, November 1964; Vol. XVIII, No. 1, November 1966; Vol. XIX, No. 1, November 1967; Vol. XX, No. 1, November 1968 and No. 2, March 1969).
The Financial Times.
The Economist.
Le Monde.

INDEX